Flying Tigers Over Cambodia

FLYING TIGERS OVER CAMBODIA

An American Pilot's Memoir of the 1975 Phnom Penh Airlift

by

Larry Partridge

McFarland & Company, Inc., Publishers
Jefferson, North Carolina, and London

Library of Congress Cataloguing-in-Publication Data

Partridge, Larry, 1936–
    Flying Tigers over Cambodia : an American pilot's memoir of
the 1975 Phnom Penh airlift / by Larry Partridge.
        p.   cm.
    Includes bibliographical references and index.
    ISBN 0-7864-0768-9 (softcover : 50# alkaline paper) ∞
    1. Cambodia—History—Civil War, 1970–1975—Personal
narratives, American.   2. Food relief—Cambodia—Phnom Penh.
3. Partridge, Larry, 1934–   . 4. Flying Tiger Line.   I. Title.
DS554.8.P39   2001
959.604'2—dc21   00-48214

British Library cataloguing data are available

Cover 1: Tiger 783; Cover 4: DC-863, C-130, and the C-46.

Manufactured in the United States of America

*McFarland & Company, Inc., Publishers
    Box 611, Jefferson, North Carolina 28640
        www.mcfarlandpub.com*

Contents

Contents

Preface

The story of the Flying Tigers began in 1941 when the call went out for pilots and ground support personnel to join Claire Chennault's American Volunteer Group (AVG) in China. U.S. Army, Navy, and Marine Corps personnel took leaves, answered the call, and went on to impress the hell out of a demoralized America and the Japanese Empire while finally affording some relief to the beleaguered people of China.

When World War II ended, a Flying Tiger pilot nurtured an ember as he made his way home. Gathering other Tiger veterans, ground support, and pilots about him, Robert W. "Bob" Prescott carefully fanned the ember and rekindled the AVG spirit by starting the Flying Tiger Line. From very humble beginnings, this venture became the largest airfreight company in the world. Bob's spirit never flagged as his nucleus attracted a group of men and women who had in common an appetite for adventure, a lively curiosity, and a love affair with aviation that allowed them to breathe real life into what some would call mere machines.

The Flying Tiger Line eventually became simply "Flying Tigers," but the mission never changed. "Can-do" and "Anything, anytime, anywhere" were not just words to us but a real credo that we all took seriously. This helped turn a profit and also applied when Tigers took on humanitarian projects. The Tigers' list of relief missions is a long one involving natural and man-made disasters that occurred at points all over the globe. This book is an account of the man-made crisis that took place in Cambodia and South Vietnam during the month of March 1975.

While we took part in this adventure Bob Prescott's only order to us was: "Do it! Do it as well as a Tiger can, but keep an eye on your tail!" Can and do: two of Bob's favorite words.

1

Too soon, in 1978, Bob Prescott left us forever when he flew the final flight west. Again too soon, his (our) airline ceased to exist except in spirit ... the Tiger Spirit.

Recently, while chatting with a Hawaiian Airlines captain, I mentioned I was retired from Flying Tigers. He smiled and respectfully said: "What a wonderful club you guys had." I couldn't agree more.

On March 25, 1975, I left Saigon, South Vietnam. Now I have finally turned a skimpy diary and my memories into a book. The "diary" I kept was just a collection of notes that were quickly jotted down on a scratch pad at the end of each day, but my memories are strong. As I knew my notes were for public consumption (press) I was careful not to step on toes, breach security, or be politically incorrect. The conflict, Flying Tigers, and many of the actors are now history ("Lord Jim" Winterberg, for one, passed away in the spring of 1997 at his home in Alaska). So I can see no reason to withhold the more interesting side of this story.

Some may say I've overdone the drama and trauma, and of course, those who shared the "pleasures" of combat will accuse me of suppressing it. Technically, I shouldn't use the word "combat" as we were officially listed as noncombatant personnel, but nobody mentioned that to the people who attempted so many times to do us harm. What "noncombatant" meant, in our case, was we weren't allowed to shoot back.

We quickly learned that it really *is* better to give than to receive. After all these years have passed I'm still sensitive to certain sounds. Recently, while my wife and I were shopping at a warehouse store, an employee slammed the door of a large walk-in freezer nearby. It took until the next day for my "fight or flee" systems to back down!

When you first enter into a hazardous situation, the tried and true "It ain't gonna happen to *me*" attitude allows you to ignore the danger. But daily exposure erodes this imaginary shield to "maybe it will" and then to "it is going to happen to me!" However, by that time you have assumed responsibility for the lives and limbs of others and you find it very difficult, if not impossible, to do the sensible thing and flee.

Popular films about Southeast Asia and its troubles have managed to ignore the most affected people—the middle class. With a few exceptions, this was the group of gentle and ambitious men, women, and children with whom we (the Ricelift pilots) had daily contact.

This material is as fresh now as it ever was. Locations, languages, and causes have changed, but nice and innocent people are still being caught up in the vicious crossfires of ethnic, religious, and political hatred. This account is a story of aviators and airplanes but is also about these people and the extreme frustration we experienced during the so-called wars in South Vietnam and Cambodia.

The book is arranged day by day. At the beginning of many days a paragraph in *italic* text describes events that actually took place on that date. It is interesting to compare this to what we *thought* was going on. The spread between the two rapidly narrows as we move along. It's hard to believe how uninformed we were, but even in Saigon, just 125 miles southeast of Phnom Penh, the three monkeys (see no evil ... etc.) were alive and well.

When I left Saigon I expected to return in two weeks, so I just said, "See you later" instead of good-bye. This book will be my closure and a way of finally saying good-bye to the many people we tried so hard to help.

Prologue
25 March 1975
(Part 1)

After a month of high tension, Jim Winterberg and I were nearly overwhelmed by normalcy as our company van dropped us off in front of the terminal at Tan Son Nhut Airport in Saigon.

Enjoying a warm, sunny spring morning, the crowd seemed almost festive as good-byes were exchanged and a few smiling tears were shed. The good feelings were not quite real though, as things were rapidly going downhill in South Vietnam. Beneath the smiles you could see dark shadows of the disease called "harsh reality" setting in.

We were headed for Hong Kong on the first leg of our journey home, a couple weeks of rest, then back to the fray.

The porters at the entrance had a "bucket brigade" going where maybe ten of them would take turns carrying your bags, each demanding a tip. I was lucky as I had a fistful of Italian lira in my flight kit. I gave each a 100L note and my bags zipped right through. I wondered how I would placate them when I returned, but that turned out to not be a problem.

We boarded the China Airlines 727 and sat in silence waiting for the doors to close. The air-conditioning was running but doors were open and with almost all the passengers aboard, it was getting a bit warm and humid.

The stewardess, a lovely Chinese lady, had noticed the Flying Tiger stickers on our kits and curiously asked if we knew anything about the airlift into Cambodia. Jim answered her question by saying: "Ma'am, we are the airlift." I assured her there were others involved but we were the first pilots to start the "Ricelift" out of Saigon. "You guys look pretty tired," she said. "Was it bad?" We talked about it.

After about 20 minutes a young oriental man, wearing a blue co-pilot uniform and a large bandage on the left side of his neck, boarded by way of the rear "air stairs." Right behind him a person on a stretcher was placed in the aisle near the rear of the airplane. The only time I had ever seen a more heavily bandaged person was in the movie *Catch-22*. The wrapping revealed only slits for the mouth and eyes and the left arm was sticking up as if frozen in the middle of waving at someone. An attendant sat down beside the stretcher.

Our stewardess friend said the patient was a Chinese pilot who had been severely wounded in Phnom Penh and was on his way to Hong Kong for special surgery. "Do you know anything about it?" she asked. Jim turned and stared out the window, leaving me (in the aisle seat) to answer her question.

They had been blown off the runway right in front of us as we landed in Phnom Penh.

I had a sour taste in my mouth as I quickly related the story and she silently mouthed "Oh no" as she looked back at the captain of Blue 46 covered by layers of gauze and plaster. I saw respect and a bit of awe in her expression.

After departure, the seat belt sign was turned off and I went back to where the co-pilot was seated. He looked up at me and I said "Blue 46?" He nodded. I pointed at myself and simply said "Nancy." He offered his hand, I shook it, then he let go and looked back down at the floor.

I returned to my seat where the Steward was now sitting. He had been talking to Jim about our experiences and was obviously impressed. He stood with a very serious expression on his face and shook my hand. After I sat down he went forward to the galley then came back with two plastic cups filled with about half Snappy Tom and half vodka.

Jim soon succumbed to his "liquid breakfast." I held on for a while, closed my eyes and thought about a zillion things while listening to a baby crying somewhere behind me.

Our Chinese angel offered me a refill but I declined. Closing my eyes again, I ran my thoughts back to the beginning of March.

1 March 1975

At 31,000 feet above sea level a Flying Tiger DC-8-63 airfreighter effortlessly levitated almost 150 tons of airplane and cargo to the west. The crew of this magic machine: Captain Andy Chambers, Second Officer (Flight Engineer) Jim Winterberg, and the First Officer (Co-Pilot), myself.

We were a bit late leaving Manila and ahead of us a red sun was just kissing the horizon as we crossed the South China Sea on our way to Saigon, South Vietnam. The sky was still warmly lit at our altitude but looking down at the surface you could easily see lights marking ships and fishing boats. Ahead, the lights of coastal villages were also coming into view. Far off and ahead to our right (northwest) several flares flickered a sickly yellow to remind us we were approaching a country divided by political conflict and coveted by its northern neighbor.

It had been a smooth trip so far and we were feeling mellow as we swapped stories about this and that. Andy told of overhearing Bob Prescott, president and CEO of our airline, describing Tiger pilots as being like seagulls. "All they do is eat, squawk, and poop and he has to throw rocks to make them fly!" After a good chuckle we prepared for our descent and landing. We were planning to spend about an hour on the ground then fly the last leg of the day to Bangkok. There, with a couple of days to kill, we were looking forward to a nice seafood dinner accompanied by plenty of ice-cold Singha beer.

I would never have expected that two of us would spend the next 26 days flying in and out of hell.

Everyone assumed the conflict in Vietnam was slowly winding down but there was no doubt in anyone's mind Cambodia was having real problems. The U.S. had pulled all military aid to that country and the

Captain Ted Brondum.

Khmer Rouge (communist) rebels, led by a psychopath named Pol Pot, were taking full advantage of the situation. After we parked on the Tiger ramp, station manager Gary Kangieser and Captain Ted Brondum came into the cockpit. They told us the Khmer Rouge had completely surrounded Phnom Penh. The airport was still open but was now within range of rebel artillery, and normal air traffic had come to a halt. There were at least one million refugees as well as residents in the city and starvation was rapidly approaching.

Rice by the ton was available from USAID (United States Agency for International Development) and Tigers had assigned an airplane, but Ted needed a First and Second Officer to make up his crew. Would Winterberg and I volunteer? We could stop any time we wanted to (more about *that* later).

Under the circumstances, neither of us felt that "no" was an option.

2 March 1975

Cambodia: *The Khmer Rouge (KR) have increased their strength around Phnom Penh to approximately 80,000 men. They are as close as three miles to the north and ten to the south of the airport. Other than serious and at times deadly harassment by government (FANK) ground-attack fighters they have total control over the area. Starvation and malnutrition are daily facts of life (and death) in Phnom Penh.*

It was 4:00 AM and the phone beside my bed was really being rude. I answered and someone from our office told me that transportation would be in front of the hotel at 5 AM. In Room 210 at the Caravelle Hotel in Saigon, I wondered what had happened to my two-day lay-over in Bangkok—my cold beer, my seafood dinner. Even though the window was wide open and my room overlooked Tu Do Street, one of Saigon's busiest, there was almost total silence. I remembered curfew ran from 11 PM to 5 AM. No wonder I was sleeping so soundly. I went into the bathroom, and the biggest cockroach I'd ever seen went scooting behind the toilet. One of my kids could have used it for a skateboard! I'd do something about him (her?) later; I had to get ready for my first day at war.

When I hit the lobby at 5 AM our van was waiting. It had a special sticker that allowed it to be driven during curfew. Scratching and yawning, we got aboard. First stop was "Steve's Place" for breakfast.

The first thing you noticed at Steve's was the security guard, a skinny, old (very old) guy who looked like he'd break if you tapped him on the shoulder. There were two things that belied that first impression, though: sharp dark eyes and an M-16 with a long clip.

He obviously knew his business and although we never became friends, I am very happy I was never on his enemies list.

The second thing that grabbed you at Steve's was the food. Breakfast and his cheeseburgers were about the best I've eaten anywhere. A black American, Steve got out of the military in Saigon. He married a local lady and opened his restaurant. It became a kind of hangout for ex-pats and riffraff like us. The pool table had seen its best days, but the food was great and the beer was cold.

Years later, I saw the bailiff on *Night Court* and said "That's Steve! Wife and all." If you read this, Steve, I hope you take that as a compliment.

We pressed on to Saigon's Tan Son Nhut Airport and passed through the fairly tight security, arriving at the Flying Tiger offices. After doing all the paper things and checking weather we were driven to our airplane, N783FT. She was loaded with 48 tons of rice and just enough fuel to go to Phnom Penh and back with a small reserve. Start, taxi, and takeoff were routine but then the fun began.

We had to circle Saigon several times to reach the magic altitude of 12,000 feet before setting out across country. That's a safe altitude if someone on the ground wants to pop off a rocket at you.

We continued our climb to 15,000 feet and tuned the radios to communicate with those on the ground at Phnom Penh. The remaining distance was only 90 miles so we made contact right away with "Tailpipe Bravo," the command post at the airport.

Unfortunately, the first words we picked up were: "All bunnies, incoming!" "Bunnies" referred to all aircraft that were on that radio frequency and "incoming" meant artillery, rockets, or both were hitting the airport. Artillery was represented by captured (made in USA) 105mm howitzers, rockets by the very mean 122mm, and a light antipersonnel type about the size of a five-foot piece of downspout pipe, the latter two made in communist China. Ted had been told that if an incoming rocket was going to be a hit-or-near-miss, someone at Tailpipe Bravo would usually see it falling, giving everyone a few precious seconds to get behind or under something.

The 105mm artillery was dangerously different in that it gave no warning! If all was quiet (no airplanes around) they sometimes could hear a round go by. But if it had your name on it you would never know what hit you. An added attraction for us flying types near the airport were SA-7 surface-to-air missiles with heatseeking guidance (they would lock onto the hot exhaust gases of an aircraft's engine and explode on contact).

Phnom Penh (Pochentong) Airport

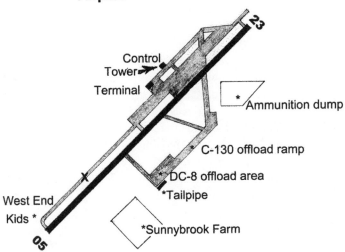

This first trip wasn't as hectic as it could have been. Captain Brondum had gone up twice the day before with another outfit and carefully observed the goings on while taking notes. The one thing that did kind of confuse the issue was the shelling was now light enough to allow most of the usual air traffic to come and go again. This was great for moving goods and people but there was little co-ordination between all the different operators, both military and civilian. There was a genuine antique airplane, about the same as Amelia Earhart's, flown by two crazy French guys (we ended up calling them Cheech & Chong) who would come and go as they pleased without *any* radio contact. Even as Frenchmen, they had to have been smoking something strange to successfully ignore what was going on all around them.

Cheech & Chong were by far the kindest titles we bestowed upon them.

Radio talk:

"Tailpipe Bravo, this is Tiger 783 … 20 miles southeast … inbound … 15,000" (feet altitude).

"Tiger 783, Tailpipe Bravo … descend at your discretion … be advised that there is traffic all over the place—high, low, fast, and slow

... watch it... contact Phnom Penh tower on one eighteen one" (118.1 was the radio frequency for the control tower at Phnom Penh's Pochentong Airport).

"One eighteen one ... Tiger 783."

"Phnom Penh tower this is Tiger 783 ... 15 miles southeast ... inbound ... passing 12,000."

"Tiger 783 this is Phnom Penh tower ... you are cleared for a visual approach to runway 23 ... please do not fly over the Palace but stay tight ... area across the river is hot." (Visual approach means there is no formal landing system in effect. The rest says that the good guys would shoot at you if you flew over the Royal Palace and the baddies would get you if your turn was too wide over the river.)

"Understand Tiger 783 cleared for visual to 23 ... we have the Palace in sight."

"Tiger 783 this is Phnom Penh tower ... land your discretion runway 23 ... please contact Tailpipe Bravo now."

"Tiger 783."

"Tailpipe Bravo, Tiger 783 turning final for 23 ... we have two fighters about a mile ahead."

"Tiger 783, Tailpipe Bravo ... roger the fighters ... they are T-28s landing and they know you're behind them ... they'll stay out of your way ... they should be turning off just as you touch down."

"Tiger 783 ... thank you."

"All bunnies incoming ... north ramp ... got that Tiger? ... you'll see some smoke off to your right, you want to go around?"

"Um ... we just saw two hits by the terminal, is that it?"

"Roger."

"We'll land okay ... Tiger 783."

After the landing and while we were rolling out, two more fighters took off behind us, roaring right over our heads. Wow! We arrived at the unloading area in front of the bunker called "Tailpipe Bravo" manned by several Americans and a contingent of Cambodian government military personnel. The military people were referred to as FANK: Forces Armees Nationales Khmeres.

As there was no ground equipment for starting or electric power, we had to leave number three and four (right side) engines running. A chap from the bunker brought the Cambodian unloading crew on board. Shortly after, crap started to hit the fan.

The airplane's nose was slowly going up! Normally there is what is called a tailstand installed when the airplane is being loaded or unloaded. This keeps a shifting center of gravity from causing the tail to settle to the ground, at best embarrassing, but in our case this was very serious. If it happened now the airplane would have to be slowly unloaded by hand from the rear of the cabin until the nose wheel returned to earth.

Meanwhile, we would be blocking the ramp and giving the enemy a nice target to try to hit for an hour or so. A decision had been made to leave the stand off to allow the airplane to move at any time but apparently someone had fouled up in the training department.

The American that brought the crew to the airplane was running his own school of weight and balance by literally screaming at the men. "You miserable f---ing brown idiots! You stupid little ---holes, can't any of you slanty-eyed idiots understand English?!" (This is English?)

As the nose moved up again, Jim exploded out of his seat and headed aft.

With the two engines running and radios to monitor, at least one of us had to be in the front office at all times. I looked at Ted and he motioned for me to follow Jim. I was in time to see him step in front of a forward moving pallet of rice (each pallet weighed about 5,400 pounds) and yell at everyone to just stop!

His fierce expression and loud voice did the trick.

A little quieter, he motioned for the pallet to be moved forward but not offloaded. At that, the American crew boss stepped up to Jim and told him to "get the hell out of the way, this is *my* crew!" The look on Jim's face was downright frightening and you could see his jaw working. Surprisingly, Jim moved close to the man and spoke quietly. I saw the man's face pale and he quietly left. Jim then turned to the Cambodians and patiently explained the problem using a stick and hand signals. It took about five minutes and everyone started doing it right (they probably wondered why anyone would have designed the original routine so obviously dumb in the first place).

Now they would replace the pallet just offloaded with all those behind before offloading the next one. A piece of cake! Much to our relief, it was soon apparent that they hadn't understood a word of what that foul-mouth freak had said to them.

We asked Jim what he said to the guy. He said he made up a story about just getting out of prison for killing someone and he wouldn't hesitate to do it again if this jerk didn't immediately get the hell off *his* (Jim's) airplane!

The offloaders finished and Jim gave each a cold can of pop. He made about 20 new friends in just a few minutes. We never did see this so-called crew boss again and assumed he'd gone somewhere else.

Now we had something new to worry about. While the unloaders were happily doing their thing Jim went out and gave the airplane a quick once-over. When he came back he mentioned that the brakes were still very hot. This was caused by landing a heavy airplane on a fairly short runway on a hot day. If we were going to take off and spend some time at a cool altitude this would not be a problem, but after the short flight back to Saigon the brakes would still be hot and the risk of blowing a tire would be very real.

The typical family car carries around 30 psi in its tires. The DC-8-63 main wheel tires used 200 psi and if the internal temperature reached a high enough point, the tire would explode with the force of a sizable bomb!

In each main wheel there is a simple but 100 percent effective device called a fuse plug. This is merely a hole in the wheel rim filled with a solderlike metal that melts when a certain temperature is reached. When this happens, the air in the tire is released and the tire is now considered "defused," no longer capable of exploding.

This "safe blowout" nearly always results in a very expensive tire being damaged beyond repair. But considering the alternative, it's quite acceptable. What is *not* quite acceptable is a flight crew that doesn't avoid this problem if at all possible.

Normally, the solution would be to spend an hour or so on the ground but that was totally out of the question as Tailpipe Bravo had just broadcast another "all bunnies incoming." The hits were still over by the terminal but... We cranked up and went after deciding to leave the landing gear down until we leveled off at 16,000 feet. Approaching Saigon, we had to maintain a minimum of (the magic) 12,000 feet until 10 miles out, so at 15 miles we extended the landing gear. At 10 miles we dropped the flaps and coasted on down for a gentle landing. Touchdown was made at the minimum safe speed with the nose high. The nose was held up as long as possible along with the engines in reverse. By doing it this way we had no use for regular brakes till we turned off at the end of the runway. This technique (used widely by the military) would be startling to a load of passengers but as we only had a load of "Cambodian air" aboard we were free to play a bit.

This profile worked so well that we used it on every flight during the operation now known as "Ricelift."

After we parked I put my hand on a brake assembly. It was warm but touchable. Grant Swartz, our maintenance rep in Saigon, walked up and tried the same "touch test" on all eight brakes. Turning to Ted, he asked, "How the hell did you do that?" Ted briefly explained and Grant remarked that our procedure not only worked but the nose-high landing and rollout was so pretty he almost shed a tear.

To Grant, the most (only?) important things in life were airplanes, high-performance race cars, and ladies. He was one of the best mechanics I've ever had the pleasure of being around.

Grant told us that Flying Tiger maintenance sent him 30 main wheel tires because "we

F/O Larry Partridge.

would be blowing a lot of them." We (Tigers) never blew a single tire due to excessive heat during our Ricelift. Many were changed because they would get so badly cut by shrapnel, but Grant was proud to say that his pilots were so good during this operation that he seldom changed a tire on a Tiger DC-8 that didn't have air in it.

How "good" we were can be argued, but it felt nice to have a man like Grant refer to us as such.

After just one flight it had become obvious that we were going to have to adopt some new rules and methods. At first, Ted was going to alternate the legs he and I flew. In other words, he had flown into Phnom Penh on the first leg and now I would do the honors on the second round, just like a regular airline trip. Now he had new thoughts. Enemy action, traffic conflicts, or both could (and did) require some very quick and nonstandard command decisions to be made. So now he would fly all the legs into Phnom Penh and heat up the brakes. My specialty would be to fly the return legs with a light touch, like the one just completed, and make the equipment happy again.

Did I take his decision as a slight against my abilities? No way! Before Ted came out with this, I had been trying to think of a tactful way to suggest the same setup to him.

Offloading the plane.

Second and third flights were about the same except the temperature got up to about 85° by mid-afternoon. Offloading was going smoothly and we acquired a Cambodian "boss man." He was a nice guy and spoke fluent English. He was with us for the duration.

Jim popped into the cockpit and said: "Larry, you've got to see this" (Ted was already watching out the left side window). I went to the forward entrance door (just forward of the cargo door) and saw an amazing show. The Cambodian offloaders had refined their routine until it resembled a ponderous, dangerous, but beautiful ballet!

They had positioned a wheeled, hydraulically activated ramp at the cargo door of the airplane. One end of this ramp was adjusted to be level with the threshold of the cargo door, and the other end, about 20 feet out, was slightly lower to give it a downhill slant.

Approaching the bottom of this "hill" was a huge forklift with its forks placed to be just below the lower edge of the ramp. A pallet was pushed out the door and almost three tons of rice hit the rollers on the ramp and quickly shot into the waiting arms of the just-arrived forklift. A second forklift moved into position as number one put its load aboard a well-used flatbed truck and the beat went on until the offload was complete. This could have been easily set to music! Jim quickly handed out cold water or pop to the gang as they filed off the airplane.

After restarting engines number one and two, the tower cleared us to taxi to the runway and proceed quickly to runway 23 at the northeast end. Just as we started up the runway, two T-28 fighters landed facing us and turned off on the terminal ramp to await our passage. This was definitely not standard procedure for a peacetime airport but somehow it seemed safe as all the pilots involved were highly skilled and on top of the situation. This made me wonder if we pilots sometimes rely a little too much on ground-bound control and let our own resources slip a bit.

Then came the exception! Phnom Penh tower had just cleared us to take off. As we started rolling, guess who plopped down right in front of us? The French "retards" in their Lockheed 10. They very quickly squirreled off to the right at the terminal ramp and got out of our way so we could continue the takeoff, but it was very close.

We were level at 16,000 feet when we passed by Neak Luong, a small city 35 miles southeast of Phnom Penh on the Mekong River. Without an airport of any size, this city was normally supplied by road or by ships and barges using the Mekong River. Now, the Khmer Rouge completely controlled river and road, and two "landmarks" highlighted the location of Neak Luong: the burned-out hulk of a small freighter lying on its side in the river and Bird Air C-130s circling the city as they air-dropped food, medical supplies, and ammunition.

We couldn't have known at the time but when Neak Luong finally fell, with the exception of some who were young enough to be "re-edu-cated," every one of its 100,000-plus people were systematically mur-dered.

As we ended our first day on the job with another gentle, brake-saving arrival in Saigon we had a lot to think about. When we arrived back at the Caravelle Hotel we met Maria for the first time. She was a lanky 13-year-old streetwise tomboy selling newspapers on the front steps. Kind of pretty, you could see that she was going to bloom into a real rose. Winterberg bought a *Stars & Stripes* newspaper and she turned to me. I asked Jim if he worked the crossword. When he said no I told Maria that I'd just read his when he finished. That's when I learned that I was a "cheap sumbitch!"

From then on, I spent the extra quarter. She became a big part of our lives and we all loved her dearly, our own "daughter of the regiment."

A quick, unremarkable dinner and it's off to bed we go. Not a bad day's work for new guys.

3 March 1975

Damn that French-style telephone! If I have to be aroused this early I prefer that it be done gently. Why do Europeans feel the telephone is so important that it warrants having a bloody fire alarm for a ringer?

At least the French didn't opt for the double ring that the Brits seem to enjoy.

4:00 AM again, there goes that silly cockroach again, and no I don't have time to mess with him (I decide for no particular reason that it is a he) again. New problem ... I discover that French-style toilet paper is not only made of 120-grit sandpaper but it also stretches! You try to use the one-handed snapoff and you end up with 47 feet of it on the floor!

Knowing about this and the fire-alarm telephone I think I have discovered why the French are so grouchy, especially towards Americans ... they're envious of our TP! As you've probably guessed by now, I wasn't in a very pleasant state that morning. I still hadn't realized that there were far more serious irritants than bad TP and loud telephones.

Except for the fact that I had sausage instead of bacon with my breakfast, this morning was a rerun of yesterday until our first "all bunnies incoming." Tailpipe Bravo had stopped giving the location of the hits (east ramp, west side, etc.). Someone had pointed out that this could be valuable information for the KR as they aimed nasty things at the area. As we sat on the ramp unloading we could see the KR were trying to do their job as hit after hit thumped into a small farm about 400 yards off to our right and forward a bit. That's a clean miss, but the way they are hitting in the same small area (called grouping) worried us a lot as an adjustment in our direction would have been deadly.

Making light of a dark scene, we named the little farm "Sunny-brook." Silently, we wondered about the family that had once lived there. Were they still alive? One can usually come up with some reason a warring faction does this or that but blasting a gentle little farm to bits while trying to destroy an airplane full of food?

I guess there are times when all else fails and war happens, but it seems Pol Pot and his band of merry halfwits were going out of their way to make this an especially cruel one. Looking back, I think that we were witnessing a small sneak preview of the "killing fields."

One of the Tailpipe Bravo guys came into the cockpit and sat in a jump seat just as Sunnybrook took another hit. He shook his head. "Bastards," he muttered. I asked him if anyone was going hungry yet. After giving me a funny look he answered by telling us that Phnom Penh was "going hungry" two months ago and it was literally starving now.

That bit of information was just sinking in when he changed the subject by pointing out an old couple on the ramp and told us their story. Probably in their seventies, she had something in her apron and he was carrying a small pail with a handle. The "something" in her apron was sand and his pail held thin tar. Every time an incoming round pecked a small hole in the ramp they would quickly fill it with sand and tar (a regular crew patched the larger ones). They just showed up one day and started filling holes while everyone, military and civilian alike, assumed that someone of authority had allowed them into the area. Questions were finally asked and it became clear that they had just quietly arrived on their own. This caused a big row among the Cambodian troops who were supposed to be enforcing a super-secure perimeter around this ramp.

The Old Couple just ignored all this and stayed on the job they created while shouts were shouted and fingers were pointed. Finally, everyone cooled down and after it was decided that they were not KR agents, an officer asked them where they lived. The Old Man stood quietly while she gestured toward a small pile of belongings behind Tailpipe Bravo. Using scrap corrugated sheet metal, some troops assembled a lean-to and the Old Couple had a humble home again. Their "pay" for the job was whatever spilled rice they could sweep up plus handouts from Tailpipe Bravo.

I asked if they could be from Sunnybrook Farm. He shook his head and said the residents of Sunnybrook were still there, buried in a shallow grave. As our off-load finished our friend stood and said: "Keep up the good work, unless something changes, your rice is the only rice any of these people are going to get."

Back in Saigon after this first flight of the day, we were driven to the Flying Tiger office complex to get our initial briefing by a USAF Colonel assigned to oversee the operation. Col. C. was a graying, slightly overweight gentleman who, at first, seemed competent enough. He carefully explained and described what we would be doing, seeing, and hearing. We listened politely even though it became obvious that he had never been anywhere near Phnom Penh, and of course, we already knew what we would find there.

I also have to mention that although he spoke as if he was in charge and knew it all, he wasn't successful in hiding the fact that he was reading notes that were lying on his desk!

"Any questions?"

I had to open my big one and ask if he knew that we had already been there and done that. His answer was an amazing: "Of course ... any more questions?"

I think it was Capt. Brondum who asked what we were to do if we went down in Khmer Rouge territory and survived. Col. C. again sneaked a peek at his notes and said: "Make contact with them as soon as possible, act friendly, show them your Department of Defense IDs (mine said I was a Colonel), and follow their instructions."

Thinking of the communication problem involving the offload crew in Phnom Penh, I asked if they could speak and read English and was told: "Of course, they aren't barbarians." (?)

I hadn't been aware the language people understood determined their "barbarian status."

By now, we were of one mind in thinking that Col. C. would be the last person to look to for leadership during this airlift. Later, we learned he did not volunteer for this job and this was probably the last place in the world where he wanted to be assigned. He had a short time to go before retirement and apparently was put here in the meantime just to keep him busy.

Three more flights about the same. Poor Sunnybrook Farm gets punched all day. Someone said if the farmer was alive and could return after the war he could forget farming and open an iron mine.

During lunch (Steve's Place cheeseburgers) I mentioned my cockroach. Ted and Jim had dozens of little ones scampering around their rooms that seemed to thrive on the spray the hotel had furnished. It didn't take too much thought for me to realize that my one big guy had claimed territory and was probably eating the little ones like popcorn. I decided he could stay and named him Hiram (doesn't mean a thing ... just popped out).

After I passed that on, Jim reached over and felt my forehead while Ted stopped chewing for a second and gave me a strange look. I said "It's possible." Jim agreed but said: "You don't have to name the damn thing!"

During our last flight of the day, the scheduled flight from Manila came and went leaving behind a large tote (fiberglass box) labeled "COMAT contents: SM Oil for Tiger 783." After we parked and shut down for the day, Grant Swartz bundled us into the van and told us about this mysterious box while he drove us to the office. He said he would open it as soon as we got there.

Ernie Miranda, our station manager in Manila, had sent it and although we all knew that COMAT meant "Company Material necessary for operations," the term "SM Oil" stumped everyone.

As we came into the office, a small crowd had gathered and during speculation about the contents of the tote, someone mentioned whatever it was it was cold as the box was sweating and a puddle had formed around the base.

Grant cut the straps and we helped him lift the lid. After a long, hot day spent sweating in flak jackets while picking cotton out of our mouths after every bang, we thought we'd died and gone to heaven when we saw dozens of bottles of San Miguel beer rolling around in ice water! Any beer served like this would have been wonderful but San Miguel, from the Philippines, is one of the world's best! Wherever you are now Ernie, thank you! bless you!

One last note before we leave the airport. World Airways thought little of our "slow" flight profile that only allowed a maximum of four flights a day. They believed that by really pushing the envelope they could do six! They would land in Saigon, use maximum braking to turn off on the first taxiway possible, taxi at high speed (more heavy brake use), and zip with a hard turn into the loading area. Almost every time, Grant would look on in disgust as he spotted at least one tire flopping around airless. In the meantime, we would come plodding in like the proverbial tortoise, reload, and depart while they made Grant swear and Goodyear happy.

After "borrowing" some rolls of American toilet paper, we headed back to the hotel. We shared the streets with swarms of blue Renault taxis and two- or three-wheeled gadgets with either human or gas power all blended with thousands of people on foot. One had to wonder where they all went at night during the silent, empty curfew.

This time, I was first to buy a paper from Maria. She turned toward Jim, who was looking the other way, and I told her that he was going to read mine when I finished it. The look on Jim's face was something else when, right out of the blue, she loudly informed him that he was now the "cheap sumbitch"!

After a shower and fresh undies we met in the lobby and ventured out to check the local food supply. We found a quiet "Mom and Pop" place on a side street not far away that served simple European country-style lunch and dinners. I had a large bowl of split pea soup, salad, and whole baguette with lots of butter ... all delicious. This little place became one of our favorites. We thought about the gang at Tailpipe Bravo and realized that being an aviator while doing a war certainly had its advantages.

We took a pleasant walk around the area then returned to the Caravelle to get our rest for day three. Between my room and the stairs to the lobby was the CBS/AP/UP news office. It was always busy and looked interesting so I decided that some day, if nobody minded, I would poke my nose in and see what was going on.

After I let myself into my room, I turned on the bathroom light and there sat Hiram. He was sitting on the rim of the tub casually cleaning his wings and feelers while apparently ignoring me! These bugs must be able to read minds. How else would he know that I had decided on a hands-off policy? Life was getting more interesting by the minute.

I woke up around midnight and lay there listening to the silent curfew. The window was open as usual and I noticed three dim flashes from somewhere outside. Curious, I sat by the window to look out. After over a minute had passed I heard three "bumps" and knew that somewhere to the west someone was being shot at by a very large gun. In roughly that same direction I saw several flares seemingly suspended in the air. One could tell they were far away as they were just above the horizon and flickered dull yellow instead of the usual steady super-bright white. How strange to feel so lonely and peaceful in the middle of a large city in the middle of a war. Three more flashes and a while later ... three more "bumps." Oh well, back to bed and sleep so the sadistic phone can have its fun.

4 March 1975

United States: It appears that the current administration in Washington D.C. is still clinging to the naive belief that Pol Pot is waging simple warfare and will be open to negotiation with Khmer Republic leader Lon Nol. In reality, Pol Pot wants the death of Phnom Penh and its people. The longer his actions can be called "war" the longer he can avoid the title "murderer."

I knew it was impossible but I could have sworn that 4 AM was coming around every 18 hours! At least it sure felt like it. Hiram now sits on the pipe behind and above the toilet and watches while I brush my teeth.

We were advised that breakfast (sweet rolls, coffee, juice, and milk) would be waiting for us at the Tiger office. Before that, our first stop after leaving the hotel would be the CIA (Air America) office at the airport for another briefing. The building was strange in that it resembled a giant freezer painted dark grey (we called it the fridge). The entry had a thick, insulated, and no doubt, armored door. Then a short dim hall, a copy of door number one, and we emerged into a brightly lit "toy shop."

A very "adult" toy shop, it had all kinds of examples of mankind's gentle nature. A little open mouthed we gaped at Chinese assault weapons, an SA7 ground-to-air heat-seeking rocket, a 122mm artillery rocket, lots of Russian guns and grenades, and various other items.

A pleasant and competent looking gentleman greeted us and went right into the lecture. It was interesting when he got to the SA7 missile and told us that if we were unlucky and attracted one, it probably (I hate that word when it's used around airplanes!) would not put us down as our engines are suspended below the wings, not built-in such as a fighter or helicopter. After familiarizing us with these things we would be seeing from the wrong end, he went on to other lore that would be handy for us to know.

Had we been advised that, the night before, a Khmer Rouge artillery spotter had been captured while trying to slip onto the airport? He had a portable radio and apparently was going to hide out on the field and give aiming instructions to the shooters! This was really bad news. And no, we hadn't heard about it yet.

Had we been told what action to take if went down in enemy territory and survived the crash? We said yes but what we were told didn't sit well and went on to repeat Col. C.'s instructions.

This "pleasant" man began to redden and take on a not-so-pleasant expression. He had two scenarios: If we went down on the Cambodian side of the border we were to take our emergency radio, get away from the airplane, and try to find a secure place to hide. As soon as it became known that we were down, CIA would dispatch choppers to locate and rescue us if at all possible. He went on to point out that we were *obviously not* Khmer Rouge and this meant a mandatory death penalty on the spot! Even if someone there could read your ID it would happen only after he pried it from your cold, dead hand.

Second scenario? If we were down on the Vietnam side we would be picked up by helicopter if necessary or, if we could get to a road and a village, a local would either bring us in or call for help. Viet Cong? As we were civilian they would probably just avoid us. Contrary to popular belief we found that CIA people generally were pretty square as long as you were away from the power-hungry crowd in and around their home office.

We had our quick and dirty breakfast and launched for Phnom Penh. As we climbed above Saigon we admired a beautiful line of thunderheads to the northeast. Old pilot's saying: "Thunderstorms and campfires have one thing in common. They're both beautiful unless you're in them."

The new radio procedure was to call the tower first instead of Tailpipe Bravo. The tower people were trying to overcome the traffic problems and the sooner they knew you were around the better. I set the frequency and braced myself for the waterfall of chatter as each pilot tried to convince the tower that he was more important than any other on that channel.

Silence ... thick, heavy, silence! We had multiple radios and I knew that they couldn't all fail at once ... could they?

"Phnom Penh tower this is Tiger 783 ... 20 miles southeast ... inbound ... 15,000." Silence.

"Phnom Penh tower, Tiger 783 ... one eighteen one." Double check the radios...silence!

"Phnom Penh tower, Tiger 783." Nothing.

"Phnom Penh tower ... Phnom Penh tower ... this is Tiger 783." Something's wrong ... try Tailpipe.

"Tailpipe Bravo, Tiger 783."

"Tiger 783, Tailpipe Bravo." Whoa, what a relief!

"Tailpipe Bravo, Tiger 783 ... about ten out passing 10,000 ... no contact on the tower"

"Tiger 783, Tailpipe Bravo ... the tower had a problem a little while ago ... I guess we are the tower now ... good news is that you're the only airplane around at the moment ... cleared to land runway 23 your discretion ... incoming nil for about 30 minutes now ... you were not advised to return to Saigon?"

"Tailpipe Bravo, Tiger 783 ... negative on the advice ... understand cleared to land 23 ... our discretion."

After we arrived at the ramp we were told that the tower (not the normal glass tower, which had long been abandoned, but a truck with radios and three or four people) was now history along with the people in it. We were not told on the way because of the timing of our take-off and radio frequency changes. We'd just talked with these people yesterday and now they're gone? We said little to each other while we sat, not quite stunned, but ... well what the hell did we expect anyway!

As Mr. Rogers would say: "Can you spell war?"

All traffic is now halted except lift aircraft, fighters, and CIA helicopters that were doing a real job moving wounded and innocents out of the hottest areas.

Aircraft remaining and their loads (some of the loads are educated guessing on my part):

Out of Saigon

Tiger 783	rice
World DC-8	truck parts, fuel oil, and some rice
Airlift International (AI)	fuel oil and rice

Out of U Tapao, Thailand

Bird Air C-130s	ammunition to Phnom Penh. Ammo and food to Neak Luong

| Trans International (TI) | aviation grade gasoline and parts |
| Blue 46 | meat, canned goods, and some fresh vegetables |

We flew trip two of the day without much in the way of conversation. I think our nerves were getting a little raw. Incoming was incoming again and was more accurate than ever. We heard lots of big ones and saw a few on our ramp!

You can't begin to imagine the sound this stuff makes. You actually feel it more than hear it as the shock wave passes ... Thump! .... Then, if a close one, the thin rattle of shrapnel bouncing off the airplane. We got two of those close ones as we departed Phnom Penh for the third time and reluctantly decided to call it a day. Three out of four ain't perfect but it was a hell of a lot better than nothing.

When we left Saigon for this third flight we were able to work up a little smile as we saw Grant playing with World's hot wheels again. Now on our way back, we heard World call Tailpipe Bravo to say they were on the way into Phnom Penh! Tailpipe Bravo answered right away and strongly recommended they take their load back to Saigon and try again tomorrow due to the accurate and frequent incoming now taking place.

It was so bad they issued a standing warning to "all bunnies" that would only be lifted when things improved. World answered they had only made one trip so far and would like to "sneak" this one in. We got on the horn (radio) and backed up Tailpipe's warning but the only response was: "What's wrong Tiger, can't take the heat?"

After we parked at Saigon we heard they had been hit hard. They really had no choice other than to try to get back to Saigon even though their hydraulic system was gone and control surfaces were badly punctured. We waited on the ramp and peered through the evening haze hoping to catch a glimpse of them. Finally, fire trucks sporting sparkling red lights moved into position and we saw the airplane turning on final approach. The landing gear was down but with no hydraulics they would have to use minimum (reserve) braking. Grant seemed happy that for once he wouldn't have to worry about blown tires!

The landing looked good and they were able to return to the ramp on their own.

What a mess! Hydraulic fluid all over everything and holes (some quite large) everywhere. Well, they did get that load into Phnom Penh but it would be a while before they could do it again. We hitched a ride to the office.

Our ride to the hotel wasn't ready yet so I decided to see what Col. C. thought about today's events. His door was closed and my knock wasn't answered. So, as this was Tiger property and there were no "private" or any other signs posted, I tried the door. It was not only unlocked but unlatched as well! I went in, turned on the light, and went to what we called the "big picture."

Col. C. had a large map of the Phnom Penh airport overlaid with clear plastic that he used to keep track of the action. Using colored grease pencils he would place an X where each piece of incoming landed. The legend at the bottom said black indicated the 122mm rockets (big), brown was for antipersonnel (bad), orange the 105mm artillery (ugly) and red stood for a hit with casualties (very bad and ugly).

I assumed Col. C. had not been in at all that day as the only marks were brown and all in the open air market north of the terminal.

Being helpful, I added my input. Two reds by the tower, several browns all over the airport, two blacks on our ramp, and a tight group of blacks in Sunnybrook Farm. I turned off the light, closed and latched the door (which didn't have a lock), and went out front where our ride had just pulled up.

Back at the Caravelle we noticed Maria wasn't around but were told she had left us three papers at the desk. I wasn't feeling too frisky so I told Ted and Jim not to wait for me as I was going to try a short nap before dinner. A short nap? ... I woke up at 11:30 PM! Because of curfew I was going to have to do without dinner tonight. I wasn't really that hungry anyway but I put junk food on my list of things to have around.

I sat looking out my window a while but about all I noticed were some flickering yellow flares to the west. No big guns tonight. Lonely and feeling a bit sorry for myself, I went back to bed and immediately fell sound asleep.

5 March 1975

Wake-up call as usual but we're told to take our time and have a good breakfast as we were going to be a little cautious about going into Phnom Penh this morning. We would go only after Tailpipe Bravo gave the word that things were back to normal (?). This *is* beginning to seem normal … is that normal?

At the office we were met by Gary Kangieser, who told us Col. C. was in a real snit. Someone had broken into C.'s office and had altered an "official document." He and his little helper, Capt. C. (yes, also C.), promised to have somebody's head on a platter.

Gary asked if we had noticed anything unusual the night before and I simply said: "The door wasn't locked." Gary's eyebrows went to the top of his head while his eyes rolled.

"You? I know you don't like the guy but why not just stay away from him?"

I said I was only trying to be helpful and how could I "break in" when the door wasn't even closed?

Gary walked away muttering something about having enough problems already without my "help!"

I went to Col. C.'s office and knocked on his door. He answered with a brisk "come" and I went in. As I was explaining what I had done and why, I noticed that the "big picture" had been wiped clean except for the brown marks at the market. He accepted my apology and explained that I wasn't a "trained" observer in these matters. I felt like saying I had just finished "on the job training" and my final test score was 100%, but discretion reared its head and I bit my tongue.

Then he did something that became his trademark: When things got tight for Col. C., he would pick up a phone and answer it. A dead phone! I considered myself dismissed and quietly left his office.

Back in our lounge, I spotted Jim taking a nap and Ted reading a book. Ted had mentioned earlier that as a pilot with the Royal Canadian Air Force during WWII he had flown supplies (including rice) from India to guerrillas in Southeast Asia. No wonder he seemed so calm about it all.

I just couldn't relax and enjoy this bit of tranquility so I decided to wander out to the airplane. It was about a half-mile walk so I had time to think about Col. C. He had little control over our operations, and I was sure the Khmer Rouge couldn't care less about his "big picture" and where he put his little Xs. So why had I come so close to getting into a "pissing contest" with him? I came to the conclusion that if anything, I should feel sorry for him and I promised myself I would stay out of his way from now on. Once in a while I found the promise a little hard to keep.

It was already 75 or 80° out and as soon as I reached Tiger 783, I went to the insulated cold drink dispensers that were set up for the ground crews. Ah ... icewater or iced tea ... I guessed I'd have the iced tea. No cups. Check in the airplane? No cups! Now I really wanted my cold drink. A group of Vietnamese loaders were sitting in the shade under the airplane and one of them noticed my plight. He said someone had gone for more cups but hadn't come back yet. He fished an aluminum pop can from a trash bag and proceeded to rub the top against the pavement in circles. About a minute later the top came off and after a quick rinse I had a very nice cup, popular logo and all. Thank you sir! I sat near the loaders under the wing, and although I didn't understand a word, listened to their soft pleasant-sounding conversation while I savored my hard won cuppa.

The peace and quiet didn't last long. Grant Swartz drove up, dismounted with his crew, and after telling me that Tailpipe Bravo had invited us back, brought the auxiliary electrical generator to life. While it settled to a throaty purr the unit used for our starting air supply gave out a loud "poot ... phooot" as it was checked. I went to the cockpit and requested our clearance from Saigon center. Ted and Jim pulled up in the van. As Ted came up to the flight deck (with lots of paper cups) Jim did a quick walk-around inspection of the airplane. We were on the move again.

That line of thunderheads was still there to the northeast. Still beautiful, but seemingly a little closer than yesterday. We hoped aloud it wouldn't get close enough to cause a problem. Surely Mother Nature wouldn't side with the likes of Pol Pot. The weather had been kind so far, perfect if you overlooked some haze and a few clouds.

"Tailpipe Bravo, Tiger 783 … 20 (miles) southeast … 15,000 (feet) … inbound."

"Tiger 783, Tailpipe Bravo … cleared all the way down your discretion … only other traffic right now are fighters … they know you're inbound and will watch out for you."

"Tailpipe Bravo, Tiger 783 … understand cleared to land … thanks."

"Tiger 783, roger … incoming very shy today."

"783."

It was a warm, golden afternoon as we arrived at the ramp and waved back at the "Old Couple" as they took a short break from sweeping and dabbing the pavement. We listened to the rattle … thump … clank … whirr … thump of the offloader's ballet and looked at Sunnybrook Farm while it enjoyed some well-earned (if only temporary) quiet. I silently wished to God that there was something I could do to really help these people. Flight number two was a rerun of this one except the Bird C-130s rejoined us in the traffic pattern.

Back to the hotel where Maria waited to see how her first credit account was going to work. We took our three papers and owing her for the three she left for us the day before I handed her two dollars expecting her to keep the change. She took that, frowned and held out her hand asking for another quarter. I hesitated, then thought what the hell and gave her the coin. Maria then gave each of us a quarter and reminded us that you can't divide 50 cents by three. Good grief, child! What little sanity Pol Pot left us with she almost got, but the laughter really felt good. She gave us her "have you been drinking already?" look and pocketed her dollars.

As I mentioned earlier, Maria became a real part of our gang and I should describe her more thoroughly. She said she was 13 years old. Tall for her age, she was on the slender side. Her "uniform" consisted of faded jeans, worn tennis shoes, and a tee shirt, all squeaky clean. Short, pretty, black hair and a beautiful smile when she cared to show it. She talked often of her mom and little brother but seldom mentioned a father. I had the feeling he had been in the military and was either missing or dead. She and her family were good Catholics and she often chewed on us for not attending church on Sundays. A bit of a tomboy, if the words "girl's dress" were mentioned, she would react like Dracula when shown a crucifix. Did she survive? *Are you reading this, Maria?*

After saying hello to Hiram and cleaning up a bit, I joined the guys (they also slept through dinner last night) and we headed for our special place. French onion soup, salad, baguette, and butter. Wonderful! Then off to an early shot at getting ready for day five. No show out west again except for the ever-present flares. A whole day without a bang! What were we going to do for excitement?

6 March 1975

Cambodia: From a volunteer M.D. in Phnom Penh: "It's worse than I expected. The conditions that I've seen have been pretty bad. I've been helping with the malnutritioned infants. I also assisted on some surgery last night. We did an amputation on one of the soldiers, amputated his arm. The soldier's ten-month-old daughter also had her left arm amputated. As you know, the families follow the soldier/father into the battles and live near them."

Something woke me at 3:30 AM and although I tried to get back under I didn't make it. I thought about some real rest and wondered why it was taking so long to get at least one more crew here to give us a hand. I'm finding out when you get really tired (exhausted?) you don't sleep well. Odd. The phone was cheated out of its sadistic pleasure as I was awake and ready for it.

Conversation was not too lively. When three guys live like Siamese triplets for five days there isn't a hell of a lot that's new and exciting to talk about except maybe the weather. It was already very warm and sticky and we agreed our flights should be a little longer so we could enjoy the air conditioning. We also agreed that a lot of people in Phnom Penh would gladly have shared our "problems" so we dropped that subject and retreated to private thoughts again.

When we arrived at the airplane Grant gave us a tour of the tires. In Phnom Penh the Old Couple at Tailpipe Bravo were doing a pretty good job of picking up shrapnel on our ramp but there was a lot of it laying on the taxiway and on the runway. This made the tires look as though some demented vandal had been attacking them with a small but very sharp knife. Grant said if we wanted he would start changing them during our reloads today but he also mentioned they had checked the depth of the cuts and he felt we could safely get a few more days out of them.

When he assured us they (the tires) would be closely watched by his crew we went along with his thoughts. Grant had to order extra nose wheel tires from our maintenance base in Los Angeles. Headquarters had anticipated hot brakes and main tire blowouts but hadn't thought about shrapnel being a problem.

We received our clearance and taxied through the muggy air to Saigon's runway 25. As we lined up we could see our old friend, the line of thunderstorms, still slowly marching in our direction. It was about ten miles to the northeast and there was an occasional flicker at the base. Actually, it might have been kind of nice if it passed through and gave some relief from the heat.

Ted pushed up the power and soon we had lift-off. N783FT was running beautifully. Through all the takeoffs, landings, and stuff in-between, we hadn't even suffered a burned-out light bulb!

Thank you, Douglas. Thank you, Pratt & Whitney. Thank you, Grant and crew. Any worries we may have had did not include our airplane.

Shortly after we were off and climbing, Saigon center called to tell us Tailpipe Bravo wanted us to slow as much as possible. The AI DC-8 was having a minor offload problem and was going to be late vacating the ramp at Phnom Penh. We "rogered" that and proceeded to loaf our way up-country.

On initial contact with Tailpipe they said the problem was fixed and the other aircraft would be departing shortly ... no problem, our usual spot would be all ours when we arrived. Incoming was very infrequent. It was humid but the ground was dry and every time the enemy popped artillery or launched a rocket it made a dust cloud. The fighter pilots could easily spot this, so after every round they (the enemy gunners) had to quickly vacate that area or risk losing their lives, or their equipment, or both. When they had some rain or wind to move the dust we'd be in trouble again.

We were on final approach to Phnom Penh's runway 23 as the other DC-8 took off and headed for Saigon. Land, taxi in, park at Tailpipe Bravo, shut down number 1 and 2 engines, wave at the Old Couple, offload, restart 1 and 2, taxi down the runway, do a u-turn, line up, power up, and we were off and headed back to Saigon. Not a single bang ... piece of cake!

While we took on a new load of rice and refueled we decided that as long as the shelling was so light we would roll all the way to the end of the runway after landing at Phnom Penh. Until now, to keep our exposure as a target to a minimum, we had been braking hard enough to turn off directly onto Tailpipe Bravo's ramp. Coasting on by to the end and taxiing back would reduce wear and tear by quite a bit. Being as nice as possible to the airplane reduced your chances of a critical failure of some kind stranding you in a hostile area.

Approaching Phnom Penh for our second flight of the day we made our usual radio call.

"Tailpipe Bravo, Tiger 783 … 20 southeast … inbound … 15,000."

"Tiger 783, Tailpipe Bravo … active runway is 23 … traffic is a Bird C-130 just landing, T-28s, and Blue 46 … Blue 46 just called 20 out so you'll be way ahead of him … cleared for approach and landing runway 23 your discretion … incoming very light."

"Tailpipe Bravo, Tiger 783 understand cleared to land 23 … we'd like to roll to the end and back-taxi … will this fit with your traffic?"

"Tiger 783, Tailpipe … it looks good for now … we'll keep you posted … if you do, please watch out for the kids at the west end, they like airplanes and get a little close."

"Tiger 783."

Kids? My mind chews on this for a bit. *They allow kids at wars?*

"Before landing checklist is complete." *Of course they do stupid, haven't you ever watched the news?*

"Speed and sink rate look good Ted." *Maybe they should rate wars like movies … this one could be R-17, or maybe X?*

"Nice landing! Spoilers are up." Jim called out reverser status and I called 80 knots. We have returned to earth.

As we approached the end of the runway we saw them. There were 20 or 30 little urchins that appeared to be anywhere from two to seven or eight years old running toward us. Their "uniform" consisted mainly of tee-shirts … period! Watching them bounce around in the weeds with their "goodies" exposed made me want to cross my legs.

We felt like the winners of a championship ball game as they jumped up and down while clapping, waving, and smiling. They did get uncomfortably close but I think the horrendous noise put out by our engines limited their approach. Those closest had stopped and instead of waving were covering their ears. A row of shacks made up of scrap lumber and corrugated metal sat about 200 yards north of this end of the runway and that, we could safely assume, was where these little guys lived.

Of course, it was unanimous we'd call them the "West End Kids." Tailpipe told us the west end had never seen an airplane as big as ours, close up. We thought of another reason to avoid this area while shelling was going on: We didn't want to draw fire to the west end and its wee residents.

Blue 46 told us he would land while we were on the runway but it wouldn't create a problem as he would turn off at the terminal ramp where his (civilian) offload area was. While we made our way back to our ramp we watched them land and Ted mentioned he had more than a few hours flying C-46s. This particular one was in beautiful shape and it seemed a shame to expose it to the hazards of combat.

While our offload was under way Jim went aft and watched. He was getting along so well with the entire crew that Ted and I decided to give him a title ... "Lord Jim." At first, he was a little embarrassed by such a lofty label but I described the story behind the name (he hadn't read the book or watched the movie) and he decided maybe it wasn't such a bad thing after all.

It stuck and from then on our Second Officer from New Jersey had a touch of class.

"Lord Jim" Winterburg.

Flight number three was a carbon copy of number two but four got a little hairy. I was the acting pilot on this last flight of the day from Phnom Penh to Saigon. We had just extended the landing gear at 12,000 feet and were about 15 miles out when Saigon center advised us that we had traffic (another aircraft) at ten o'clock (to our left and slightly ahead) five miles (distance away from us) altitude unknown. We didn't think anyone would be up here to our left as we were just skirting a sheer cliff of solid dark cloud on that side (the line of thunderstorms). Again … traffic now ten o'clock and three miles. That means we are heading for the same spot but the information is strictly two-dimensional, and as this other guy was not talking to Saigon on the radio, we felt almost certain he was one of the many helicopters zipping around at low altitudes in the area.

We were now ten miles out of Saigon so I closed the throttles, set full flaps, and started down. Ten o'clock and one mile! *Damn!* A little edgy, I started a gentle right turn to open the distance between us and the wall of clouds. *It's got to be someone down low.* Ted, Captain Brondum, is a soft-spoken, gentle Viking who seldom got too excited about anything so when I heard "Larry, Roll Right!" I instantly rolled to the right and looked left. There was a South Vietnamese Air Force C-130 coming out of the clouds straight at us, so close I could make out the two pilots staring back! Tightening the roll to near 90° I let the nose fall through and we ended up pointing nearly straight down!

Back pressure … be gentle but hold positive Gs … rudder? … try to center the ball … yaw damper is helping … good.

Obviously we had avoided a collision but now I had to get good ol' 783 back to an attitude where she was comfortable.

Hold the back pressure … speed is building and flaps have blown back to 35 … center the ball … speed is stabilizing … good … nose is coming up and speed is going down … great! … flaps are back at 50 … great!

Large airplanes don't like being handled this way but as we were empty of cargo and low on fuel, she was light, and with flaps and gear extended, dirty, so our speed didn't build all that fast. A few warning lights flickered (fuel pressure, etc.) but soon all was under control again. Throughout this strange maneuver Ted had his hands and feet lightly on the controls but, assuming all the right moves are being made, it's best to let the flying pilot finish what he started. Thanks again, Douglas!

To this day, my scalp crawls when I think about this incident.

After we arrived at the ramp we told Grant about our cheap thrill. He said the C-130 we encountered was probably out of Bien Hoa, a military base about 15 miles to the northeast of Saigon. He added that, because the war situation was getting critical in South Vietnam, the military were getting a little casual about observing the normal rules of safe flight. We decided to treat each substantial cloud as if it had something hard in it and give it as wide a berth as possible.

I was about a quart low so I was delighted to see that Ernie Miranda's daily shipment of "SM Oil" had arrived from Manila. I made my way to the container and two of the most appreciated cold bottles of beer I'd ever had went down my hatch. If you really want to enjoy a cold beverage just have someone scare the "whatever" out of you on a hot, hot day, then knock it back. That's stress management!

Once again we arrived back at the hotel too late to greet Maria, but once again our newspapers were at the front desk. Tired, and as we had eaten well for lunch (Steve's burgers and fries), we opted to give it up for the day. I got to my room (no sign of Hiram), nibbled some potato chips, read the paper, and crashed. This time I stayed down all night.

7 March 1975

South Vietnam: Equipped with Soviet made T-34 tanks, North Vietnamese troops of the 316th and 10th divisions are quietly moving out of Cambodia and gathering in the hills west of Ban Me Thuot and Duc Lap. Just 150 miles north northeast of Saigon these towns are thought to be well out of harm's way but the first shock of reality is about to be felt by the South.

One good thing about skipping dinner is it improves one's enjoyment of breakfast. Taking care of that at Steve's Place we then motored on out to the airport and the office. Rumors that the North Vietnamese were preparing to storm across their border and capture Hue were countered by: "They'll get their butts kicked" or "They wouldn't try, they're not nearly strong enough," but I still felt apprehensive. Just a few months ago, the Khmer Rouge were described as being "a bunch of disorganized teenaged clowns." I think that was mostly true except for the "disorganized" part.

The thunderstorms we hoped would cool things off a bit just quietly dissipated leaving behind little puffy clouds and lots of heat. The temperature was forecast to be in the mid-nineties and that turned out to be just about right. The good news was, as I said earlier, this was not a good thing for the Khmer Rouge artillery people. It seemed that they had taken the day off, as I think there were only two rounds of incoming all day! The Cambodian fighters kept up their busy schedule looking for whatever targets that might show themselves.

While we were offloading, these fighters would taxi close in front of us on their way to refuel and re-arm and we usually got a wave and a thumbs up. I don't know how they can smile while sitting in an unairconditioned "greenhouse" on a 95° day while fighting a war. I think I could do the job but I sure as hell wouldn't be happy about it.

In Saigon, the damaged World Airways DC-8 was parked about a quarter-mile down the taxiway from our ramp. Every day we passed it on our way to the runway and could see several people working to repair the damage. This morning we saw that a large "cherry picker" crane belonging to Pan American had lifted two men to the top of the vertical fin (rudder) to install patches over the many holes there. We noted the height and didn't envy them at all.

When we returned from Phnom Penh we looked down-ramp and noticed the cherry picker boom was no longer in sight. Grant came into the cockpit and we remarked about how quickly the patch job had gone. He smiled a bit and said to look a little closer when we passed that airplane on our way out. "You'll really appreciate how strong these birds are," he said. Now curious, we finished our checklists, started the engines, got clearances, and headed for our departure. Slowing as we passed by the World airplane we were amazed as the scene became clear. An extended brace on one corner of the crane had broken and the whole works toppled over. The boom had landed on the horizontal stabilizer (tail) of the DC-8 and was still draped over it! The force of the fall had broken the boom about halfway up and the bucket that had held the two men was suspended about six feet above the ground. The airplane didn't appear to have suffered at all!

Grant told us later there was some minor sheet metal damage but the main structure was, in fact, unharmed. After being treated for shock, the two workers quit.

At the airport in Phnom Penh a little breeze had picked up from the east and the active runway was switched to 05. Our last take-off of the day started from the west end and the kids waved good-bye instead of hello. Thankfully, they seemed to have had experience with airplanes and high (takeoff) power settings as they stayed well clear of the airplane and the jet blast. I hoped no one was hurt while gaining this "experience!" We didn't have to worry about passing too close to the Palace when we departed as the empty airplane leapt off less than halfway down the runway and after a steep climbing right turn we headed directly for Saigon.

Various factors broke our stride and we could only complete three flights. Except for the heat and our being so tired, this was an easy day but an ugly fact kept us from enjoying the respite. When things were quiet around Phnom Penh the Khmer Rouge were not taking the day off. To the contrary, they were as busy as packrats laying in new caches of rockets and artillery ammunition. When conditions improve (for them) they're going to get our undivided attention!

We leveled at 16,000 feet and shortly passed about three miles southwest of Neak Luong. The town was not quite visible but easy to locate. The markers were silent columns of smoke and a lone Bird C-130 pooping white parachutes while flying in lazy circles. Drifting down to Saigon, we had a chance to simply enjoy the view.

There are many reasons pilots love their job or hobby, and one of them is being able to see the world from such a lofty perch. The low, afternoon sun was washing everything in that soft golden light so peculiar to Southeast Asia and it was hard to imagine the conflict going on almost three miles below. It would have been nice to stay up for a while and soak in some peace and beauty but Saigon control wouldn't hear of it. "Tiger 783 cleared to descend and maintain 12,000 … speed your discretion." Oh well, under the circumstances, a few minutes of reverie was a lot better than none. SM Oil here we come!

Ernie's SM Oil had indeed arrived and along with it word that another crew was due in tonight. I might have a chance to spend some quality time with Hiram.

On the way to the hotel we talked about the possibility of doing a little sightseeing. We'd been here a full week now and hadn't seen a thing except a hotel, two restaurants, two airports, and the inside of our eyelids. We asked our driver if the blue (Renault) cabs were expensive and he assured us they were dirt cheap.

That was good because we soon found out they were so small we usually had to order one apiece. France's answer to the VW, they somehow managed to build it larger on the outside and smaller on the inside.

Maria met us at the hotel and collected exactly what she was owed. She seemed satisfied she had taught us well. We mentioned we might have some time off soon and she volunteered to show us around the shops in the area. So now we had a pretty, savvy interpreter who was also our friend. With her grasp of math and no-nonsense manner we doubted that any merchant would even try to get the best of us.

She turned out to have one fault. If she didn't approve of your taste in art or whatever, she would lose interest and you soon found yourself without her help in bargaining. Small price.

Someone had told us about the buffet at Brinks hotel just down the street so we gave that a try. Not bad. They served pretty much basic American-style and the price was right. With full tummies our sixth 4 AM wake-up call in a row quickly got to us and we slogged back to the Caravelle and bed to get ready for number seven.

Hiram showed up to sign "good night" with his feelers.

8 March 1975

Wake-up call! The voice on the other end told me the new crew is here and will meet us in the lobby. We will fly the first trip while they observe then have the rest of the day off! Somehow it doesn't seem right to share our adventure even though it means some much needed rest. What an odd reaction to good news.

Flying Tiger pilots wore a very nice uniform; a crisp, light blue short sleeve shirt with striped epaulets to show our rank (Captain, First Officer, or Second Officer), dark blue slacks, shiny black shoes, and the typical airline pilot's hat. Sweating under a flak jacket and worrying about slinking around in the weeds while evading capture caused us to change *our* "uniform" to casual shoes, jeans, a simple tee or polo shirt, and a baseball or bush hat to keep the sweat out of our eyes. All three of us dressed as usual this morning without even giving it a thought. Of course, the three new guys were all in regular uniform.

Instead of "Hey, glad to see ya" or "How you doin'" we just stared at each other for a long moment while we saw ourselves as we were a week (only a week?) ago and they wondered if we were going flying or fishing.

On the way to Steve's it didn't take long before we were chattering like a bunch of teenage girls after a dance. We answered most of the questions by saying we would show them instead of trying to explain in detail. That's when we realized just how different this operation was and how much we had learned (and aged) in only a week. I started to mention my cockroach but decided they weren't ready for that yet.

When we arrived at the restaurant we pointed out the old man with the M-16 and said that he was there to make sure that no one tried to leave without paying. I think the guys believed it.

At the Tiger office we had another pleasant surprise. A flightline mechanic from our Chicago base was here to ride the flights with us. He would keep an eye on the machinery and if there was a problem would either fix it or evaluate things and let someone know what we needed when we (hopefully) arrived back in Saigon.

His name was Gregory Slack and he was a competent, pleasant person to have around.

We gave the new crew a repeat of the CIA briefing and warned them to listen politely but ignore anything Col. C. may say to them. We did the paper stuff, checked weather (the usual), and set out for Tiger 783. The airplane was loaded and fueled with the ground crew standing by so after the checklists were read and the radios preset we called for pressure up (air) and started our engines. Saigon tower cleared us to taxi to runway 25 Left and the clock was running. Passing the World DC-8 we told the story of the Pan Am cherry picker and pointed out the tail surface being worked on.

Now cleared for takeoff we lined up on the runway, set the power, and were on our way. We did the climbing left turns until passing 12,000 feet and then pointed the nose toward Phnom Penh. The new crew had been briefed on the "bunnies" so it was interesting when I tuned the radio to Tailpipe Bravo and the first thing we heard was: "All bunnies incoming!" Our new crew chief, Greg, passed out flak jackets and no one hesitated to put one on.

"Tailpipe Bravo this is Tiger 783 ... 40 out ... level 15,000."

"Tiger 783, Tailpipe Bravo ... Neak Luong is hot with three Birds overhead ... Phnom Penh active (runway) is 05 ... right-hand pattern ... fighters have acknowledged your presence ... also one Bird just departing 05 ... he should be well on his way by the time you land" (the call at 40 miles out and the Neak Luong advisory were new).

"Tiger 783 ... Thanks."

Neak Luong came up on our left and we pointed out the wrecked ship, columns of smoke, and the Bird C-130s dropping supplies. We mentioned that 16,000 feet was the minimum altitude if we were passing directly overhead the city, but as our normal track always took us to one side or the other that shouldn't be a problem.

"Tailpipe Bravo, Tiger 783 ... 20 out ... 15,000."

"Tiger 783, Tailpipe ... Descend and land your discretion runway 05 ... we'll keep you posted on traffic."

"Tailpipe, Tiger 783 understand cleared to land 05 ... we have some new guys on board could you hold the incoming for a while?"

"Tigers came up with more crazy pilots? ... welcome guys."

"783 ... (laughter) ... not as crazy as you."

"We got a half-inch thick piece of steel to hide under ... what've you got?"

"Good odds? ... see you shortly."

Two fighters landed at the other end (head on) just as we touched down and one of the new guys yelped that we had traffic on the runway. That's exactly what I would've done a week ago but I just said they would get out of our way and a few seconds later they scooted off onto the terminal ramp to await our passage. As we rolled past them both gave the thumbs-up sign and a big smile. At the end, we did our u-turn and followed them back to the ramp. We told the guys we would try to explain some of this when we got back to Saigon.

They marveled at the offloader's ballet and I told them about the Old Couple. Someone mentioned the possibility of our rice going to the black market and not helping the people that really needed it. I explained this was being monitored closely and the rule was cooked rice was free to anyone. There were several stations set up in town that did nothing but cook rice in huge vats. Bagged dry rice could be bought and resold but only if there was enough cooked to go around.

Actually we never did get ahead of the demand to the point where any dry rice was available but I'm sure some got sidetracked. We did know that the cookers never had to stop for lack of rice, but the lines of hungry people never seemed to get any shorter, either.

With the offload finished and all engines running, we taxied out the ramp and down to the west end where our new crew got their first look at the West End Kids. A remark was made that they didn't really get as close to the airplane as was expected. We said that this was a takeoff and they respected the high power setting. After a landing was when it got scary.

Tailpipe said there wasn't any significant traffic so we did the takeoff thing and turned sharply toward Saigon. Before we switched to Saigon control we told Tailpipe to take care of the new guys and asked about the French pilots and their Lockheed 10. It was a relief to hear Tailpipe say that after a near miss, "Cheech & Chong" had returned to Bangkok and were looking elsewhere for work.

Cheech & Chong and an old Lockheed 10? That's another topic we're going to have to explain in detail.

While showing off our descent profile we mentioned clouds in the area are to be watched closely as they sometimes carry nasty surprises like VNAF C-130s. Drifting in for the nose-high landing we demonstrated the control and power settings we had fine-tuned by trial and error to make everything as safe and easy as possible.

Our main wheels kissed Mother Earth and we rolled to a gentle turnoff at the end of the runway. Making our way back to the reload area we parked, shut her down, and gathered up our belongings.

After making the new crew solemnly promise (I even checked to make sure they didn't have their fingers crossed) to be nice to Tiger 783 we wished them well, got off, and headed for the office.

I was all for a day of rest and relaxation but Jim had run into an old friend at the office and they talked me into a round of golf at the Saigon Golf and Country Club just off the airport. Ted had more "won't" power than I and he departed for the hotel. A short ride later, Jim's friend had set us up with a 30-day guest membership and we headed out to terrorize poor little white balls and anything else in our immediate vicinity.

My caddie, a slight little lady around 30 or so, was reading a book whenever she wasn't helping me look for my ball. Curiosity got to me and as I could see the book was written in English, I asked its title.

She told me she was studying for her license to practice pharmacology and had a test on Monday. She said she went to school five days a week and spent the weekends (this was Saturday) as a caddie to make a few bucks. Her book was a bit dog-eared and I promised myself when I went home for a bit, I would find some good stuff to bring back to her.

I wasn't doing too bad until we made the pit stop at the ninth hole. A couple of giant beers combined with the 4 AM wake-up had their effect. Teeing off at the 10th hole I made a casual swing and heard a loud and sharp crack. My ball looked like it was going back to the future as it started low, and leaving a trail of sparks, actually went up then sliced over a fence and zapped into a crowded bus stop! Even before it hit anyone I quickly handed the two iron to my caddie and said: "I'm through!" "I think so," she said, and we just walked and talked through the rest of the game. Whomever I hit I hope they were communist.

That was the last time I ever played golf.

After the round, Jim's friend drove us to Steve's where we had a bite to eat and a few more beers. Back to the Caravelle, say hi to Maria, and crash. It was still daylight but I crawled into bed and slept like a groundhog in December. I think it was about 2 AM when the beer I had consumed forced me up for a relief run to the potty. Then I sat for a while at the window watching far-off flares and flashes while hearing the "bumps" of those big guns. Somebody was having a lousy night.

9 March 1975

It's now 2:30 AM and I'm tired but wide awake. Seeing the dim flashes and hearing the three bumps, I wonder why three? Have to ask someone. Maybe Grant would know. It seems the big gun is busier than usual.

One reason sleep is so far away is the thoughts jumping around in my head. I called my wife day before yesterday but the connection was so bad about all I understood was that someone at Tigers had called her and told her what I was doing and that I should be home in a week or so. "Or so" was close.

That American that freaked out at the Cambodian offloaders? I wondered what his problem was. Scared! He was scared right up to the edge of hysteria, maybe a little over that edge. Even though there was frequent rotation to U Tapao, it was amazing how some people could sit, sleep, and eat for weeks in a hot little bunker while being constantly shot at and not go bonkers. It was bad enough just popping in and out like we were. I hoped he got out okay and found a job with which he was happier.

I wondered when we, the United States, were going to say enough already and kick some butt. Then my thoughts went a few years back and 340 miles north to Danang, South Vietnam: *It was about 2 AM and we had started our final approach to land when those on the ground saw a stream of tracer bullets coming up at us! All we saw was a line of gray smoke in the area lit by our landing lights. Thank God our Captain had WWII experience! He realized what was going on, switched off our lights, and called for max power. He pulled up into a climbing turn while the rest of us wondered what the hell was going on. He finally had time to explain that what we saw were tracer bullets from their front end! His quick action probably saved our lives. We circled and landed from the other direction and as we did we saw a helicopter gunship circling the spot where the enemy gun was located. He was firing so many rounds into the small spot that it actually glowed in the dark! This incident gave me my first lesson on how this "war" was being waged. I was later told the pilot of that gunship was facing possible court-martial! He did not request permission from headquarters in Saigon before reacting to our problem!*

Maybe the cavalry isn't on its way. Maybe the guy with the ball got tired of playing this game and left for good. I'm glad fire departments, surgeons, etc. don't do it that way.

3:30 AM and I had an idea. I switched on the bed lamp and took a small tool kit from my flight bag. I took the obnoxious phone apart and lightly stuffed the bell with toilet paper. Smiling and drunk with power I returned to bed and darkness.

Flash ... flash ... flash. Wait a minute and bump ... bump ... bump, most people count sheep or blessings or something other than gunfire!

I finally slipped off and slept fitfully until curfew ended and the traffic noises opened my eyes. 6 AM? Curfew must have been extended an hour. I wondered how that would affect things. I got up to pee and Hiram was sitting on the tub to greet me. Having him room with me seems to be working as I still have only one instead of a swarm of the buggers.

Crawling back into bed I managed another hour of low-quality sleep and then my phone hummed. It hummed! No bell! I have defeated the truly obnoxious telephone! I'll get the no-bell peace prize! Jim was on the other end and couldn't understand why my "good morning" sounded so cheerful. After I convinced him I was alone and sober, he suggested that we grab breakfast then go out to the country club and sit by the pool. That sounded okay so we agreed to meet at the hotel coffee shop. He said he called Ted but there was no answer.

After a rather bland breakfast we left the hotel lobby and looked around for Maria. Not spotting her, one of us remembered her asking if we were going to church on Sunday (today) so we assumed that she was attending Mass which, as it turned out, she was. When she asked us if we attended services and we answered no, she said if we fly airplanes and fly them to Phnom Penh we really should go to church and we could go to hers.

When I said that we weren't Catholic she just said, "That's okay, you be with me."

A pair of young ladies wearing the most beautiful and feminine costumes I had ever seen strolled past. I hope they were flattered and not offended by our staring while we admired the long, crisply white dresses accented by summer skin and raven hair. Later we learned this costume was called "Ao Dai" (long dress). Gorgeous!

Moving to the corner and Tu Do Street we hailed a blue Renault taxi, squeezed in and were off to the club. There was barely enough room to breathe and I wondered aloud what would happen if one of us sneezed or did something even worse. Jim said: "Don't even think about it" and I answered by saying I was sure glad he used Dial.

At least we still had a bit of a sense of humor. The driver seemed to know what we were saying and he reacted by shaking his head and smiling. How can so many of these people be so damned cheerful while sitting in such a dark shadow?

After changing into our swimming trunks, we looked for a table beside the elevated pool. We seemed to be out of luck until a nice couple offered to share theirs. Introductions were made (I hope they forgot my name, too) and a round of drinks was ordered. He was retired military, about 55 or 60 and his wife was a lovely Vietnamese lady probably in her forties. You can go anywhere in the world and find attractive women but Vietnam seemed to have way more than its share.

He had heard of our operation and remarked that "we looked sane." I still had the nitely big gun on my mind and asked him about it. It was a 155mm cannon probably firing at suspected Viet Cong units in the Mekong River Delta and it was big, the projectile being about six inches in diameter. He wasn't sure why they fired in threes but they did.

He asked if we had seen white helicopters with ICCS lettered on the side. Yes, we had, but we didn't have any idea what they were. ICCS stood for the International Commission of Control and Supervision that was set up to oversee the cease-fire between the communist North and South Vietnam. There was a big problem in that the commission was headed by communist Poland and they were showing flagrant bias against South Vietnam. If a South Vietnamese aircraft flew too close to a border they would receive a violation and a stern warning. The communists could actually fire a weapon and it was "I hear nothing ... I see nothing" from the Poles. Canada had been a member of this commission but when their long and loud protests were ignored the Canadians gave up in disgust and went home.

After enlightening us on that, he pointed to a family sitting not far from us. A man around late fortyish, a plump wife, and three kids.

The man was the Polish general who was in charge of the ICCS. They seemed to really be enjoying the good life here at a country club built by capitalists. It's odd but I had noticed this guy earlier and immediately disliked him even though I hadn't yet known his background. He had a kind of slick smugness about him that gave the impression that he knew he was vastly superior to all those around him. Neither he nor I were aware of it at the time but we were going to get to know each other quite well.

Our new friends went on to tell us that there was absolutely no hope of any intervention for Cambodia or Vietnam, and having disposed of property and things, they were preparing to leave for the U.S. Vietnam? I thought things were on the mend in this country. "Wait a few days" was his answer! Although I wouldn't abandon all hope based on the words of one stranger, this was very depressing to hear as we were already feeling the seeds of doubt before his words came along to water them.

Tigers had us paged at the club and I went to the phone. Gary said that another airplane had become available but not another crew. We were back to the 1:1 ratio and schedule starting tomorrow morning. I muttered something nasty and Gary said he didn't think I would be overjoyed by this news. What an understatement. He also said the curfew now ended at 6 AM and we could sleep in until 5 AM. I assume he said that with tongue in cheek. Heading back to our table while thinking black thoughts, it entered my mind the amount of rice flown in by us would double and that was not a bad thing for the people in Phnom Penh. Just being tired sure beat being tired and hungry.

I was sure more volunteer pilots would show up soon. When I told Jim, he gave me that "you're kidding" look but I wasn't trying to hide a smile and he decided I was on the level. As we excused ourselves to head back to the hotel the lovely lady gently shook our hands and said: "Thank you."

We "squeezed" our way back to the Caravelle and spotted Maria on the front steps. As we bought our papers she said it was too late for her to take us shopping but we would go tomorrow. When I told her that we had to fly tomorrow she frowned and said: "I hope you make lotta money 'cause you sure don' have any fun." I assured her that we'd go shopping as soon as possible but I didn't know when that would be.

Leaving her to tend to her newspaper sales I went into the lobby and saw Jim talking with Ted Brondum and Tiger Captain Bob Bax. Bob shook my hand and announced he was our new boss. They were pulling

---

Captain Bob Bax.

Ted out for a while (he would return later in time for the last act) and he would be on his way home tomorrow. We—Jim and I—could have done much worse as Bob was a very pleasant chap and a good pilot. The three of us stuffed his head with the lurid details of the ricelift and he took it all in as amazing but doable.

He said, "Larry, you're going to be the acting Captain until I catch on." I wondered aloud if we could also swap paychecks. "No but the drinks are on me until I'm trained" … deal!

Ted warned Bob that I enjoyed doing aerobatics in the DC-8 and described our near miss.

We took our chatter to the little restaurant and had another simple but very good dinner. I think Ted, Jim, and I missed having a fresh pair of ears to chew on so coffee and dessert lasted quite a while. Bob told us he bumped into Col. C. at the office and got a "slightly" different story. There had been very little activity around the airport at Phnom Penh and it was Col. C.'s opinion this meant the Khmer Rouge were on the verge of quitting the war and things would soon be back to normal.

Later, Bob would say that the three of us stared at him as if he had just sprouted a third eye. We described Col. C.'s tendency to slip into a fantasy now and then and explained that the Khmer Rouge were actually restocking for their next fireworks display! If there was a best time to leave for Phnom Penh, it was during a heavy show of "incoming" which would usually peter out by your time of arrival. The enemy either ran out of set-ups, had given away their positions to the FANK ground-attack AT-28 fighters, or both.

Bob had been on the road for a while and we were dragging so we all wandered back to the hotel and split for our rooms.

10 March 1975

South Vietnam: NVA troops, many armed with flame throwers, and tanks of the 316th and 10th Divisions spilled from their hiding places at precisely 2:00 AM. Their first objectives? The city of Ban Me Thuot and the town of Duc Lap.

5AM, an extra hour of sleep and a civilized telephone! Little things *do* mean a lot. Actually I did feel pretty good this AM. I wondered how long it would last.

Throughout breakfast and the ride to the airport we continued Bob's "training" and I noticed something strange. Being a pilot and a lifelong fishing nut I've never had any trouble exaggerating when telling an exciting story, but while relating details to Bob I caught myself doing the opposite! I guess the enormity of our situation hadn't totally registered yet and the plain truth was unbelievable without embellishment. Jim did a good job correcting me every time I tried this downplaying.

We passed through security and on to the already bustling office. Jim went out to Tiger 783 while I lead Bob down the paper trail. He signed the usual weight and balance form, flight clearance form, the "I have checked the weather" form, and the "I have signed all the forms" form. Arriving at the airplane, Bob said hello to Greg, and having run out of excuses, we climbed aboard and went through our preparations to go flying. Checklists complete and clearance received, I called Grant on the interphone. "Okay Grant, pressure up." (air pressure for starting the engines) "Pressure coming up Larry, all engines clear ... 3-4-2-1" (the usual starting sequence). "Turning 3."

When all four engines were running and we had our taxi clearance from Saigon ground control, I gave a thumbs up to Grant. After holding

Jim Winterburg (right) supervising activity at Tailpipe Bravo.

his wands straight up (touchdown!) he motioned smartly and marshaled us out of our parking slot and onto the taxiway. I said, "Bob are you really sure you want to do this?" He answered by saying, "I always felt we were locking them out when the last door closed, but now I feel like they just locked me in! Let's go feed someone."

"Tailpipe Bravo this is Tiger 783 ... 40 out ... 15,000."

"Good morning Tiger 783 ... Neak Luong is hot with one Bird overhead ... active is runway 23 ... traffic is Blue 46 departing ... fighters have acknowledged your presence ... check 20 out."

For a moment, I wondered how Blue 46 got there so early then I remembered that U Tapao did not have a curfew. Neak Luong was slightly different today. Along with a circling Bird C-130 and gray smoke, a column of oily pitch-black smoke had been added and as we passed by we could see an angry red-orange mass of fire at its base. What an ugly mess! Bob just stared and slowly shook his head.

"All bunnies incoming ... Tiger you'd better shorten it this time ... that one was near the end."

"Tiger 783 ... understand ... we're coming up on 20 out."

"Tiger 783, Tailpipe ... descend and land your discretion ... stay tuned for traffic advisories."

"Tailpipe, Tiger 783 ... understand land our discretion."

As I slowed for the steep descent, Jim deciphered Tailpipe's instructions for Bob: We were to shorten our landing roll as the west end had taken the hit. We were all pretty quiet as we worried about the West End Kids. Of course, Bob hadn't seen them yet but we had described them well and he felt like he knew them.

Now close in, Bob got his first look at the airport while I did steep righthand circles with the flaps down and the landing gear extended to waste altitude. Rolling straight, I pointed out the Palace ahead and to our left. Around and past the Palace I flattened the turn a bit and a 370-foot-tall TV transmitter antenna went by just to the right. I added some power and called for the rest of the checklist as the runway magically lined up ahead of us.

After a "not too bad" landing, I could say that once again superstition and good luck had defeated science and modern technology (another old pilot's saying).

I came out of reverse thrust at 80 knots and when Bob asked about the rattling sound under the floor, Jim said that it was just shrapnel being kicked up by the nose wheel tires! Later, Bob would say what really amazed and frightened him a bit was the fact Jim and I just shrugged this off as normal. Using the brakes more than I like, we pulled up to the Tailpipe Bravo exit, and as the DC-8 ground steering is controlled from the Captain's side, Bob took over while I gave directions.

The ramp "monitor" was a big guy. His job was to give us hand signals for close-in maneuvering while arriving and departing, and generally keeping an eye on things. He would stay in our sight at all times when we were on the ramp and if he spotted something amiss, would let us know. I think we called him Big John so I'll call him that now.

Big John looked like a real-live tourist with his cowboy boots, Bermuda shorts, and a cheap, loud Hawaiian shirt all topped off by a wide-brimmed straw hat! This morning he came into the cockpit and asked us what we knew about Ban Me Thuot. We hadn't heard a thing. Apparently one of Tailpipe's radio receivers had become active very early in the morning and a FANK Lieutenant who understood Vietnamese had listened in. He said the panic-stricken voices were screaming

Big John at Tailpipe Bravo.

something about NVA tanks and flame throwers just west of Ban Me Thuot! Knowing this city was only about 150 miles north of Saigon … we were interrupted by Cambodians shouting and the radio announcing: "All bunnies … incoming!" Big John said "Oh oh," Jim offered a more rich four-letter word, and Bob said: "What's the matter?"

Answering, I opened my mouth and … Thhummp! … said: "Shit!" Shrapnel rattled against the airplane and Big John asked us to find out about Ban Me Thuot as he left quickly. Jim followed him out to check on Greg and look for damage. I looked at Bob and when I saw two wide eyes staring at me from the space between his baseball cap and the top of his flak jacket I wondered why I couldn't laugh. I said: "Captain Bob Bax you are now a fully fledged member of our club!" and offered small comfort by adding: "They don't all come that close."

The offload resumed and we assumed correctly that no one had been seriously hurt. Bob asked what the dues were for this club and I said: "Hopefully … nothing." He just sat, quietly thinking, until I picked up the checklist and started to go through the items.

Jim and Greg came in and said that there didn't appear to be any damage. Jim dropped a very warm piece of shrapnel into my hand. It was light but razor sharp, obviously the antipersonnel type designed to hurt people not machines. How nice. Bob lightly moved it against his flak jacket and it cut like a scalpel! Greg had crouched down beside the left main wheels and could see blast debris bouncing all over the place but nothing touched him.

Back in Saigon S/O Joe Pacini and others show off ominous "souvenir" from Cambodia.

With everything buttoned up and all four engines running we checked with Tailpipe.

"Tailpipe, Tiger 783 ... ready to go."

"783, Tailpipe ... hold short of 23 ... after the Bird C-130 departs you're cleared to back taxi to runway 23 ... traffic just reporting 40 out is Tiger 791 ... fighters have been advised."

The Bird C-130 went on its way to U Tapao and we went to the end and did our u-turn into position for takeoff. Bob called for max power and shortly after we were officially on our way back to Saigon. We saw Tiger 791 descending about a mile from us and gave them a "good morning." We didn't say anything about our near miss as we didn't want to act as spotters for the bad guys. Passing southwest of Neak

Luong we noted that the column of black smoke had thinned quite a bit and guessed that it was probably a fuel dump that had been hit.

Bob had me do the now familiar "tire-savers" descent and landing while he watched and asked a few questions. Actually, except for our near collision, this part of the operation was fun. You don't often get a chance to fly a big airplane like this as if it were a Super Cub.

We were on our final approach when the World Airways DC-8 lifted off on its way to Phnom Penh. We wondered aloud if their run of bad luck was finally over.

Our main wheels "smooched" Mother Earth and we rolled out with the nose high until the speed dropped and the nose gently did the same. Bob took over and headed for the ramp. I said: "Welcome to our war, Bob."

Properly parked and shut down, we heard the cargo door being opened along with the chatter of the loading crew. This was going to be a quick turn-around as a slot had opened unexpectedly at Tailpipe. There was room for two DC-8s at the Phnom Penh ramp but for maximum safety and minimum target profile only one at a time was allowed. At U Tapao, TIA's DC-8 had a mechanical problem and if we went back right away we could use their slot. Grant came into the cockpit with our paperwork as the reload/refuel operations got underway. We asked him about Ban Me Thuot and were surprised that he hadn't heard anything. He said it was probably just diversionary harassment that goes on all the time along the borders. I said maybe the ICCS should snap at the other side for a change. Grant put on a crooked smile and asked me if I believed that the Easter Bunny really laid chocolate eggs.

Changing the subject, he told us this time we would have a passenger. The head of the US Federal Aviation Administration (FAA), Southeast Asia Region, had flown in from Manila to observe the operation and we were the "lucky" crew to be observed. We felt like little kids about to be caught smoking behind the barn! Before we had a chance to do any soul searching or hand wringing, our guest entered the cockpit and introduced himself. Right away this gentleman explained he was aware this was a war and definitely did not want to cramp our style in any way. He knew there would be rules bent or broken and just wanted to see how we were doing without the usual standards.

We relaxed as we realized that this man was indeed a gentleman with authority and not another Col. C. Jim picked out a reasonably clean flak jacket for him and gave him a briefing on emergency exits, what to do in case of whatever, and what to expect on the ground at Phnom Penh.

With our new friend safely strapped into the jump seat behind Bob we were once again taxiing to Saigon's runway 25 Left. After a brief delay waiting for a pair of Chinook helicopters to cross the runway, we were powered up and rolling. Explaining procedures, we went through all the now usual stuff like the climbing left turns until reaching 12,000 feet and why (missiles). I called Tailpipe Charley to report 40 miles out of Phnom Penh.

"Tiger 783, Tailpipe ... active is runway 23 ... Neak Luong is hot ... no Birds overhead at this time ... traffic is AI DC-8 just departing ... one Bird to depart after AI ... one Bird in the pattern for landing ... fighters have been notified."

"Tiger 783"

Jim was relieved that our FAA man understood all of that except the "hot" part. "Hot" meant an area where active combat was taking place. He said he suspected the same but wanted to be sure as he was taking notes.

We pointed out Neak Luong with its shipwreck and columns of silent smoke and explained how the Bird C-130s would circle overhead while literally dropping "life" suspended under white parachutes. Tailpipe interrupted.

"All bunnies incoming!"

He had been told about the "bunnies" but asked what type of incoming. Jim gave him a rundown on that then it was my turn.

"Tailpipe Bravo, Tiger 783 ... 20 out."

"Tiger 783, Tailpipe ... descend and land your discretion 23."

We did the usual tour before lining up for landing and while on final approach saw a large cloud of dark brown dust erupt at Sunnybrook Farm! Right after the expected "all bunnies incoming" I said that had to be a round from a 105mm howitzer, our worst nightmare! I hoped a fighter would get right on the gunner's back and they wouldn't have the chance to fire again while we were there.

This turned out to be exactly what happened. A FANK pilot flying about four miles north of the airport was looking right at the spot when the gun discharged. This created a puff of dust to mark the target and all he had to do was roll slightly to his right, put the nose down and ... gotcha! This info came from Tailpipe after we parked. We had no way of knowing if the gun had been destroyed, but if any of the shooters were alive they were probably too busy scrambling for cover to think about firing again for a while.

After touchdown and during roll-out Jim described the shrapnel we were running over and our observer wondered why we didn't ask for a truck with an electro-magnet under it. He was sure that U Tapao had some (they're used for picking up metallic foreign objects that could damage an aircraft engine) and could send one on a Bird C-130. I pointed to a wrecked and burned-out vehicle near Tailpipe that was the magnet bearer. The man who had been driving it was dead.

The runway was just too dangerous a place to be for any length of time. This runway, he asked? He looked more than a bit concerned when I nodded.

Big John came aboard and asked about Ban Me Thuot. When we said we were told it was just VC harassment he said perhaps so as his radio receiver had now been quiet for some time. He grimly affirmed the hit at Sunnybrook was a 105 and gave us the good news about the FANK fighter pilot's quick kill.

About then, Jim came into the cockpit muttering obscenities. When asked about his problem he said that he had slipped on a cargo roller and a moving pallet ran up on his foot! He removed the shoe and sock revealing no blood and probably no broken bones but his toe was already turning blue … ouch! Someone mentioned the medic at Tailpipe but Jim shook his head and said: "Let's just get the hell out of here. I'll have it looked at in Saigon." Offload finished, we had all four running and "got the hell out," with one little hitch. Just as we turned onto the runway to go to the takeoff end, two almost simultaneous hits landed just to the right and about 200 yards ahead of us! Then … "All bunnies incoming." No kidding!

Moving right along we turned into position and I had us quickly on our way back to Saigon. One more "all bunnies incoming" and a "good afternoon" to Tiger 791 as they started their descent.

When things settled down, our FAA man asked Bob why we didn't wait to make sure more shots weren't "incoming?" Bob looked at me and raised his eyebrows. I said that, so far, the enemy shooters were too far away for real accuracy and if there was another round on its way it could have landed where we were waiting, especially if there was a spotter somewhere in the area. The only safety precaution available to us was to keep moving and increase the odds against our "winning" this lottery!

Like a fly on a dart board we had to keep our time on the target to a minimum.

We told him about our near collision with the VNAF C-130 and how we still filed an instrument flight plan but flew by visual rules when near clouds. The normal regulations were fine as long as everyone in a given area was following the same ones, but mixing methods when you can't see each other is sooner or later suicide/homicide. Too many clouds around here had hard things in them!

The company radio came to life and Gary advised us to prepare for another quick turn-around back to Phnom Penh. Before answering, Bob turned, and thinking of the sore foot, looked at Jim. Jim said he'd be okay, especially as he had Greg to help with the walk-arounds (exterior inspections).

After I did yet another demonstration of the "tire-savers" approach and landing Bob steered us to the loading ramp. Our FAA friend said he would be around all day and would see us when we came back. A well-informed, really pleasant guy.

Along with fuel and rice, a bag of sandwiches came on board. We started biting these right away as it had been a while since breakfast. Three or four days according to Bob. Our load was about completed so between mouthfuls of ham and cheese I called Saigon center and asked for our clearance. One would think it silly to go through the same ritual again and again but there was some normal traffic along our route and this had to be done to ensure separation. Coordination of the DC-8 arrivals in Phnom Penh was handled by military controllers in Saigon and U Tapao, but when airborne, the regular air traffic controllers kept an eye on us till contact with Tailpipe Bravo was established.

Clearance received, engines running, and it's taxi-time. Bob lined us up on runway 25 Left and after setting max (takeoff) power, led us on another stroll through the valley of death.

"Tailpipe Bravo, Tiger 783 ... 40 out ... level 15,000."

"Tiger 783, Tailpipe ... Neak Luong is hot with one Bird overhead ... your traffic is TIA just departing, one Bird on final, Blue 46 about to depart and the fighters have been notified ... call 20 out ... active is 23 and we advise staying short." The west end must be taking some hits again ... Damn!

"Tiger 783 ... roger."

"Blue 46, Tailpipe ... after the Bird clears you're cleared for takeoff."

"Tailpipe, Blue 46 ... roger ... a rocket just hit about 300 meters in front and to the right!"

"All bunnies incoming ... Blue 46 you're still cleared for takeoff your discretion ... thanks."

"Blue 46 ... roger."

As we passed Neak Luong an unlikely thought crossed my mind. If I ever had the chance to listen to New York air traffic control on a busy day again, it was going to be like sweet ... sweet music!

"Tailpipe, Tiger 783 ... 20 out."

"Tiger 783, Tailpipe ... traffic is a Bird departing and fighters ... descend and land your discretion 23."

"Tiger 783 ... roger."

"All bunnies incoming."

None of us said it out loud but we were all thinking the same thing. How long could Phnom Penh hold out if no substantial outside help arrived? Were we merely a life support system for a brain-dead city? Didn't our *wsponialy Polski* (wonderful Polish) general remember how the people of Warsaw were cruelly slaughtered while the Soviet army deliberately took a rest stop just miles away? If so, why is he so happy about this situation? He must be a very good communist ... a real "People's Hero."

As we turned into the offload area there was another "all bunnies incoming" followed quickly by a hit between us and Sunnybrook Farm and another, which we couldn't hear or feel, over near the terminal. Big John asked again about Ban Me Thuot, but we hadn't heard a peep. It seemed odd that we hadn't heard anything, good or bad, about that area. Rumors are usually confirmed or denied but this one was being treated with silence.

Offload was complete in just minutes, and as it was my turn to drive, I called for the checklists and prepared to take Jim and his now black big toe back to Saigon. After a Bird C-130 passed in front of us we proceeded to the runway and headed northeast to the end. The Birds dropped their loads in just seconds by lowering the rear cargo door/ramp and shoving the pallets of cargo out while moving at about ten miles per hour. As we passed his ramp to the runway he was already waiting for us to go by and as we cleared he turned left onto the runway and took off behind us in the opposite direction. By the time we had done our u-turn at the end and were ready to go he was way high to the left circling to gain altitude before heading off to U Tapao.

I called for max power and very quickly we were in a sharp, climbing left turn. Bob had noted our point of liftoff and after some quick calculations came up with a take-off run of only 3,500 feet! Later, with more careful measurement, 3,200 feet was about right and we started thinking about how nice it would be to avoid all that time spent taxiing by just turning onto the runway and going. Another old pilot's saying: "The only time you have too much gas is when you're on fire and unused runway behind you doesn't count for anything."

He was probably right about the gas but I'd bet no one was shooting at him while he was preparing to use all of his runway.

Tiger 791 squeezed in a fourth, amid very heavy incoming, but we were through at three flights completed and went looking for the SM Oil. Along with others now off duty we found our FAA guy at the trough. He spotted us, fished out three cold ones, and we all went to a nearby desk where he had his notes. He said that we had broken about every rule there ever was when it came to airline regulations, but if we went "by the book" this operation would be almost impossible to accomplish. He went on to say a state of emergency existed and as long as people were willing to accept the risks (volunteers) the mission should be continued. He had no suggestions for us as "we were way ahead of him" on writing our own rules to minimize the dangers ... "Keep it up but for God's sake know when to quit!" Then he said he had a question about the "incoming." "Don't the rockets kick up dust the way the 105s do?" Jim explained that they do but most of the launches are done with what was called a pan switch. Simple but clever, it is a shallow pan (or even a tin can) the shooter places on a crude set of metal contacts at the end of a pair of wires leading to the rocket. When filled with water the weight of the pan holds the contacts open and a battery (flashlight or whatever) is wired in. The shooter simply leaves the area and later, when the water evaporates, the contacts close and "whoosh" leaving nothing at the launch site to shoot at. If the angle is right and the wind cooperates the next step is to announce: "All bunnies ... incoming."

Back at the hotel, Maria showed real concern when she saw Jim limping with one shoe in his hand. She bawled him out in a motherly way for not being careful, and said: "Don' do it again, OK?" Jim gave her a dirty look and grumbled that he'd try. Bob had been briefed about earning the title of "cheap sumbitch" so after we introduced him to Maria he dutifully bought a paper along with Jim and me.

Jim told Bob and me that he was skipping dinner tonight and after going to his room would get the room boy to bring him a bucket of ice. He was sure aspirin and ice would do wonders for the foot and he'd see us at 6 AM sharp. I was tired as usual and after the late lunch on the airplane wasn't really hungry (I also had a sandwich and a bottle of SM Oil in my flight kit) so I told Bob that I was also going to lay low and would see him in the morning. What a first day he had!

On the way to my room I wondered why the room boys were called "boys." The youngest one I ever saw was in his forties, and my second-floor room boy, with a touch of gray hair and dressed in a uniform consisting of black slacks and a crisp white Nehru-type jacket, was a distinguished looking man who was probably close to sixty.

After the regular staff left for the day, the room boys would take their places, and while keeping an eye on things, would provide limited room service (ice, bottle of wine or beer, etc.). Due to the fact they were mainly concerned about security during a war, I thought it possible these "boys" were really military personnel in disguise. It certainly wouldn't do to have a VC infiltrator padding around inside a hotel full of local and American VIPs, pilots, correspondents, and other persons somehow involved in the conflict. I'm sure this wasn't so but it seemed like a clever idea at the time.

The CBS news office door was wide open so I paused for a look. I think this was their busiest time of the day as it was early evening here and early morning in New York. As I stood there watching the bustle and listening to busy teletypes, a man inside spotted me and motioned me in. He introduced himself as Peter Collins, this bureau's chief correspondent, and asked if I knew any of the Flying Tiger pilots that were here with the Ricelift. I told him he was in luck and introduced myself. After shaking hands with all in the office and agreeing to an interview as soon as possible, I was able to ask about Ban Me Thuot.

Except for the various machines, the office slowly quieted as my words were relayed to those who hadn't heard them the first time. Peter looked very serious as he asked: "What about Ban Me Thuot?" He paled as I described the radio chatter that was heard at Tailpipe Bravo very early this morning. He said nobody seemed to know anything other than a few weak rumors and what I had just told them was a real bombshell. Peter had sent a much-liked local photographer/correspondent to that area Sunday morning and hadn't heard from him since! I couldn't believe it because though I knew the military sometimes kept quiet about things, I thought war correspondents had their sources and always knew what was going on. The shocked expressions didn't improve when I added that Big John's radios had been silent since the first panic-laden outburst.

I apologized for bringing apparently bad news, said I was glad to meet everyone, and retreated out the door. Peter came with me and told me about the young correspondent, how talented and well liked he was and would I please keep my ears open and pass on any information that I may come upon. I promised and said I'd see him tomorrow night. Peter, his staff, and I became good friends before this mess came to an end.

Washing down the now soggy sandwich with the now warm beer, I just sat and stared out the window for a while and counted a few "bumps." When it came to guns I always thought "bang" but now I decided that "bump" was more like it.

Good night Hiram.

11 March 1975

South Vietnam: Except for a few pockets of resistance the NVA considers Ban Me Thuot theirs at 1200 local time just 34 hours after their attack began. Soon, the word will get out and the rest of South Vietnam will wonder if the final countdown has begun.

Transom: A small window above a door that can be opened for ventilation. I thought I'd better explain that as most of us haven't seen one of those for a long time, if ever. Anyway, it was 2:30 AM and the transom above the door to my room was open as usual when there was a terrific bang in the hallway. When you've been doing a war for a while, nothing gets the heart started faster than something like that.

I leaped out of bed and my first thought was that someone had set off a grenade in the hotel, but after listening for a minute I heard a male voice talking quietly to a sobbing female somewhere close to my door. Wrapped in a towel, I opened my door and saw the second-floor room boy with an obviously upset young lady. I asked what had happened, and while she glared at me, he explained that her boyfriend had gotten mad at her and threw her out of his room.

My "big bang" was a door slamming! Thinking about losing valuable sleep I came up with a few nasty things I wanted to say to this "gentleman" and asked which room she came out of. While he answered by insisting: "She won't say," I saw others also clad in towels or wrinkled pants, shake their heads and go back into their rooms.

The room boy started to talk to her again and I asked him to take her to the lobby for their chat. He told me the manager wouldn't let her stay in the lobby and the MPs would arrest her for being out during curfew (there was a nighttime MP station right outside the hotel entrance).

I told him she couldn't stand outside my door until curfew ended, I had to get some sleep! He looked perplexed and she looked like she really didn't give a damn about my sleep. There was a small couch/bed against the wall of my room opposite my bed so I told the guy to check some ID, so he'd know who she was, and tell her she could stay on that couch until curfew ended. After he passed that on she looked at me in disbelief, not because of my generosity, but obviously because of what she thought I had in mind!

I had him explain I was going to get a call at 5 AM and I had to go to work at 6 AM. She glared at me for a moment, then said: "You don' touch me at all?" I said: "No I don' touch you at all!" and asked her to please make up her mind ... I was very tired. She squeezed past me and flopped on the couch. The room boy showed a smile of relief as I closed the door and she was still glaring at me when I turned out the light...what next?

5 AM on the button. The phone hummed, I woke up and answered, and my guest said: "Don' touch me!" After I took the call and hung up I didn't say a word while I positioned my towel, gathered my clothes, locked the bathroom door (my wallet was with me), and crawled into the shower. I came back into the room fully dressed and I could see the look of relief on her face. She had probably been on full alert until now and was no doubt tired, but she had avoided a lot of problems and somehow I was glad that I had done what I did. I guessed that she was 20-something and could see that after a good night's sleep without tears she would be quite pretty. I didn't know if I would tell my wife about this or not.

I was gathering up my things when she asked my name. I told her, and then asked hers. Telling me it was Ann, I said: "Nice to meet you Annie." I was immediately informed it was Ann not Annie! I tried again. "Nice to meet you Ann," I said. She then asked: "What you do?" After I said I was a pilot she said: "Where you go?" I said Phnom Penh and she said: "Bu shit! Nobody go to Phnom Penh! ... You die if you go to Phnom Penh! ... Everybody die in Phnom Penh!" Then she calmed a bit and asked: "Why you go to Phnom Penh?" I said people there were hungry and my friends and I were taking them some food. While she thought about that, I asked if she needed money for a taxi or anything. She shook her head and as I started out the door she said ... "Larry?" I stopped and looked at her as she softly said, "Thank you." I never saw her again.

I have to stop the story for a moment to point out that if Ann (maybe An?) was a typical Saigonese she could speak and understand at least three languages, and if she says: "Where you go," that's close enough for me. Maria spoke and understood Vietnamese, English, some Chinese, and some French.

Her "sumbitch" was also close enough.

In the lobby, Bob and I could see Jim's foot was still bothering him but he said with some more aspirin and a little sympathy it would be okay. So off we went to breakfast. I told Bob and Jim about Ann, and Jim immediately took on a knowing smile. I countered that with: "I'm dead tired at three in the morning. I am expecting a five am call. I have a very angry tear-stained lady glaring at me, and you think I asked the room boy for a bottle of champagne, two glasses, and a lit candle?" "Hey, it might have worked" Jim answered. "I don't think so," I responded. "Next time I'll send her to your room."

"Hiram! Aw crap, I forgot to tell her about Hiram!" Bob looked kind of confused as Jim said: "Your stupid bug? Why would you want to tell her about that?"

"She'll kill him if she sees him, that's why," I explained.

"Look," Jim said, you've got a stranger, a freaked-out woman on your hands, and you're going to tell her you have a foot-long pet cockroach in your bathroom?"

"She would have jumped out the window and if she survived the fall, would have turned herself in to the MPs!"

Jim turned to a now smiling Bob and very seriously said that I was frigging and totally insane! Bob was laughing now and when he could, said: "Don't turn him in yet, we need his warm body on the airplane. Just don't let him play with anything sharp."

War is hell! Hiram was fine, apparently he stayed undercover until she left.

At the office a smiling Col. C. greeted us with news that the area around Tailpipe hadn't taken a single piece of incoming this morning. He really didn't get it when instead of happiness and cheers, he got groans and a sarcastic "Thanks a lot Colonel!" We hoped we could get in and out before the fireworks started.

"Tailpipe Bravo, Tiger 783 ... 40 out ... level 15,000"

"Tiger 783, Tailpipe ... roger ... Neak Luong is hot with 2 Birds overhead ... active is runway 23 short ... (new way of saying there are hits at the west end ... Mr. Rogers won't ever visit that neighborhood! Can you spell "stay down," kids?) ... traffic is Blue 46 departing, one Bird on final, and fighters have been advised of your presence ... call 20 out."

"Tiger 783 … roger."

There wasn't much smoke at Neak Luong and we wondered if there was anything left to burn.

"Tailpipe, Tiger 783 … 20 out … 15,000."

"Tiger 783, Tailpipe … cleared to descend and land your discretion … be advised there is activity across the river and downtown is receiving many hits at this time."

We stayed as high as we could during our pass over the city and saw several puffs of black smoke right in town. What a terrible thing!

On the ramp with the offload in progress Col. C.'s prediction of a nice day was busted by "all bunnies incoming." As we sat pumping adrenaline, two FANK soldiers on bicycles came by on the taxiway beside us frantically pumping pedals to get to some cover. Too late! The round hit about 50 feet (150 feet from us) beside them and both went flying. We thought we had witnessed the end of two lives but they slowly got to their feet and retrieved the bikes! Obviously stunned and in some pain from hitting the ground at around 20 miles per hour they seemed otherwise okay.

The round had hit on the pavement and although the shock wave spread in all directions the hard stuff (shrapnel) bounced up into the air. We noticed it took a few seconds to hit the airplane and when it did, it rattled down like hail instead of hissing against one side or the other. The Old Couple were next on the scene and they smiled and waved at us as they started to patch the hole.

I was gone … why was I here? Why was anybody here? Get the Old Couple, Big John, his friends, the West End Kids, and the bodies of the Sunnybrook Farm family on board and let's just get the hell outta here … forever!

I had almost totally lost the meaning of the word "normal" and my hands were really shaking. I tightly held the control wheel so nobody would notice and waited for my heart to slow down to … normal? I guessed that it wasn't just me when out of the blue and while staring straight ahead, Bob slowly and loudly recited the old pilot's advice on relieving tension, "Take a deep breath and wiggle your toes." We all laughed like idiots and immediately felt much better.

Even with the two engines running, the Cambodian boss heard us and came forward to see what was going on. Cracking a smile of his own he watched for a moment then went aft again while shaking his head. He no doubt thought we were very brave aviators. If he could have looked inside my soul at that moment he would have seen just how thin the wall was between laughing and crying.

Calming down, I blamed my temporary loss of control on a lack of sleep combined with the heat. I hoped nobody had seen anything. I knew the answers to the "whys" that had spun around in my head but how much longer could our good luck hold?

Big John came into the cockpit and said because of the heavy incoming, their supply aircraft wasn't going to make it today. All they had to eat or drink were C-rations and warm water. He asked if we "could possibly spare some coffee."

Doing better than that, we gave him the insulated coffee jug, sweet rolls, and a promise to bring something more substantial when we returned around lunchtime. Smiling and thanking us, he proudly took his booty and headed back to the bunker. When I shouted: "Don't forget the tip," he said "I'll give you a tip … don't come back!"

This time, our laughter was a little more relaxed (normal?). Offload finished, we prepared for departure with "all bunnies incoming," one at Sunnybrook and one on the terminal ramp twice interrupting the checklists.

Off for Saigon we gained enough altitude to contact Tiger operations on the company radio. After giving our ETA and maintenance status, Jim related the food and drink situation at Tailpipe Bravo and was told to "standby." Gary came on and said he had Steve's Place on the phone and would we take Tailpipe's order? Bob talked to Tailpipe and got back to Gary: "Ten cheeseburgers with everything, fries, and chocolate shakes." When he came back so fast, it was obvious Big John hadn't asked each individual what he wanted and we had a suspicion that he didn't really believe we were doing this. He would soon find out that Flying Tiger's can-do spirit applied to all things great and small.

Passing Neak Luong, we saw a new column of rich black smoke forming and I silently wondered what it would feel like to be in that situation. Little or no hope of rescue or escape and to surrender would be immediately and cruelly fatal. The only option available to the residents of Neak Luong was not to live or die, but to die today or tomorrow or, if lucky(?), next week!

During shutdown on our ramp in Saigon, an obviously angry Grant Swartz came aboard and told us that World was grounded again! As his supply was down to ten main wheel tires, Grant had refused to sell any more to World and told them they would have to find another source.

Mr. D., the owner of World, was in town and it seems he and Grant had quite a few loud things to say to each other. Mr. D. accused Grant and Flying Tigers of deliberately crippling the competition, and while hoping to make a few more bucks, were also hindering a humanitarian airlift!

Grant resisted the urge to get physical and closed the argument vocally with: "Teach your f---ing pilots how to fly and you won't need so many f---ing tires and my guys won't be busting their asses trying to make up for your f---ing missed flights!"

Mr. D. flushed bright red and apparently was at a loss for words as Grant spun around and left the office to meet us at the ramp. I wished I had been there to watch the "King" of World get his. He had a reputation of being a pushy, loudmouthed, antilabor (anyone with a status lower than his) type who thought he was the center of the universe. Good show, Grant!

We had our new load of rice, a fresh drink of fuel, number three engine running, and Bob was turning number four as the van pulled up. The aroma got us all drooling (our lunch came after this flight) as large bags were brought aboard with Tailpipe Bravo's piping hot and ice-cold orders in them. An extra coffee jug, a large cardboard box, an extra case of pop, and a bag of ice were also brought in, the entry door closed, the boarding stand removed, and without missing a beat number two engine was turning.

All starts complete, Grant sharply marshaled us onto the taxiway and what was probably the most unique fast-food delivery service ever was on its way.

Jim got on the company radio with the departure message giving our off times and ETA at Phnom Penh. When that was completed and acknowledged, Gary came on and said the cardboard box brought on with the food contained baseball hats bearing the Tiger emblem. We were to help ourselves and would we please pass them out to anyone at the Tailpipe ramp who wanted one. Greg went back to take a look and came back wearing one. It was a good-looking cap and after he modeled it for us by striking a very professional looking pose it was decided we couldn't do without so he brought up three more. Of course, Lord Jim put his on backwards.

"Tailpipe Bravo, Tiger 783 ... 40 out ... level 15,000 and we hope you're hungry."

"Tiger 783, Tailpipe ... Neak Luong is hot with zero Birds overhead ... active runway is 23 short ... traffic is a Bird departing now and

Tiger 791 departing shortly … fighters are aware of your presence … please repeat all after level 15,000?"

"Tailpipe, Tiger 783 … just asking if you're ready for some lunch."

We could hear his transmitter hum and there were voices in the background. Big John came on.

"Tiger 783, Tailpipe … they don't believe me … answer is affirmative."

"Tailpipe, Tiger 783 … roger."

If the enemy was monitoring this conversation they were probably frantically pawing through their code books to find out what horrible new weapon was about to be unleashed against them!

"Tailpipe, Tiger 783 … 20 out."

"Tiger 783, Tailpipe … descend and land your discretion … Tiger 791 is just departing and we have one Bird inbound that should be gone by the time you get here."

"Tiger 783 … understand … thank you."

On arrival at the Tailpipe ramp we were confronted with a problem that none of us had anticipated. How do we transfer all this food to Tailpipe right under the noses of the Cambodian offloading crew? War is not only very unhealthy but also very complicated.

Incoming was light at the moment so Lord Jim went aft with the large cardboard box and told everyone to stop for a moment. He then asked the boss to find out who wanted a Flying Tiger baseball hat, and after translation, every man on the crew lined up. While Jim handed out the hats, Greg and Big John transferred the "care packages" to Tailpipe Bravo. Then … "All bunnies incoming" and life returned to normal.

Pretty soon we came to realize our Cambodian ground-support people felt if it took cheeseburgers and fries to keep us there bringing in the rice, so be it! It was possible the smell of onions with an overtone of hot grease didn't remind them of home cooking anyway, but we still felt a bit awkward showing such a wealth of food. Especially when rumors of cannibalism occurring in and around Phnom Penh were becoming common.

Big John's quick response to our request for an order was explained by the fact that earlier he and the others at Tailpipe Bravo had been fantasizing about what food other than C-ration beans and weenies they would rather eat.

Cheeseburgers, fries, and chocolate shakes won hands down. So that's what he passed on to us when we asked.

These "home deliveries" increased to at least one a day as Tailpipe's usual source of daily supplies became unreliable due to the frequent and accurate shelling. Cost? Who knows? Steve's Place donated by giving a good discount on these meals and Tigers paid the rest.

If I ever apply for a delivery job at a pizza place could I say I have experience?

Offload complete, we buttoned up and started engines number one and two. As we prepared to leave we were treated to a real show. About 20 smiling people, including the Old Couple, lined up by Tailpipe Bravo each wearing their Tiger hats and giving us two thumbs up. We smiled back, opened our side windows, and between us, Bob and I returned the gesture. Our smiles turned to downright laughter as we noticed several of them couldn't really see us. They hadn't had time to adjust the head band! Why is this paragraph so hard to write?

We started our turn to head for the runway and as our friends were passing out of view we saw them scatter and pull on steel helmets (those that had them) then … "All bunnies incoming." That one did no physical harm … it landed at Sunnybrook Farm.

As we slowed to turn around at the takeoff end of the runway we saw a Bird C-130 turn to a short final approach facing us, then pass overhead just clearing our tail as he landed in the opposite direction behind our airplane. This would have scared the hell out of all of us in the good old days, but now our only reaction was to admire his skill.

After we lined up, the Bird was clearing the runway so we immediately began our takeoff. No "bunnies," but a brown cloud erupted about 300 yards ahead and just to the right of the runway! Now we heard, "All bunnies incoming … you okay Tiger?" We were passing through the dust from the explosion when Bob answered, "Yeah, we're fine" and I pulled 783 into the air. Somewhere along the way we had learned rockets gave off black smoke when they hit and the dreaded 105mm artillery's signature was brown. We were a grim-faced bunch as we all knew that, had we been at that point on the runway when the shell hit, we would now be just a few hundred pounds of dead meat in a scrap aluminum oven.

Completing the sharp climbing turn to the left, I gave 783 her head (autopilot) and let her run for the barn (Saigon). Other than the required checklists and radio calls nothing was said while we contemplated our future in this line of work. As we passed southwest of Neak Luong, Bob looked at the now huge column of smoke, slowly shook his head, and broke the silence by saying: "Poor bastards!"

That was our problem! How could we sleep, eat, live, or look in a mirror if we did the "smart" thing and turned our backs on these people?

This positive trait called compassion had us trapped and could likely have a very negative effect on our existence! Oh well, I had never won a lottery. Maybe the Khmer Rouge won't either. After all, that hit was almost 300 yards away.

The pleasure of the Super Cub approach and landing pushed the morbid thoughts to the back of my mind and I wondered if my wife would be jealous if she knew how much I loved this airplane. That's when I came up with the idea of naming Tiger 783 after my wife. She couldn't possibly be jealous if it carried her name! Phnom Penh PhNancy ... great! We were getting close to the "dirt" so I put my idea on hold and concentrated on landing. Another smoothie! It had to be. With all the practice I was getting I'd have a hard time explaining a less than good landing. Bob took over and drove us to the ramp for lunch.

I seem to be writing a lot about food in this book. After noticing this and thinking about it, I can see the only time we were relaxed and enjoying ourselves was during a meal. Even booze had been restricted unless you count the cold SM Oil.

Someday, I imagined, we were going to receive a real day off and have something other than our last meal to think about.

We were going to be on the ground for a while so we ordered lunch by radio and hitched a ride to the air-conditioned office. While waiting for our burgers the news came in that Ban Me Thuot had been attacked and taken by NVA troops and tanks! A counterattack was being set up and officials told the public everything would soon be okay. I wondered if Big John had heard this yet. I wondered about Peter Collins' Vietnamese correspondent. Things were getting thick in a hurry, and along with many others, I wondered if this ship called South Vietnam had just struck an iceberg. In an era of modern communications how could something like this sneak up on everyone?

Ban Me Thuot was a city, not some obscure little village!

Bob was in another room making up a message to our system Chief Pilot. He was asking about progress on the evaluation of using less than the entire runway at Phnom Penh for take-off. It was understandable that caution was being used as 3,800 feet was not a common length for an airplane as large as the DC-863. As light as we were and using maximum power settings (almost 80,000 pounds of thrust) we

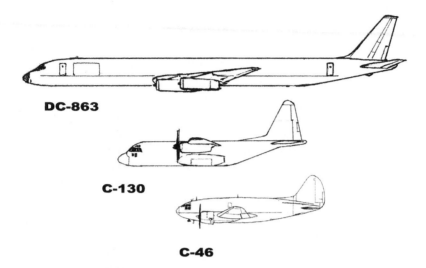

DC-863

C-130

C-46

Three of the planes most used during the time of the ricelift: The DC-863, the C-130, and the C-46.

were consistently leaving the ground by 3,500 feet or less but only after taxiing almost the whole length of the runway and turning around at the end. If we could get approval to do the shortcut we would greatly reduce our exposure to the shelling and would cease to be a challenge to the smaller aircraft that shared this environment with us. The last we heard they were trying to load this data into the simulator computers, but this was frustrating to us as we had already proved the concept except for one thing, that being an engine failure at a critical moment. Finding this "moment" during very rapid acceleration was the hang-up.

We felt 783 would do just fine on three engines at any point after 80 knots and the odds against losing an engine at such a minuscule point in time were far greater than the odds of getting nailed by the Khmer Rouge. An hour ago we had just missed a "critical moment" where we would have lost a lot more than one engine!

With a satisfying lunch under our belts it was time to get back in the saddle for our third and final trip of the day. Climbing out of Saigon we admired the afternoon gold wash over the landscape and wondered aloud if it ever rained. Of course we knew it did and one of us had information that March was typically the driest period of the year, averaging just one day of rain.

"Tailpipe Bravo, Tiger 783 ... 40 out ... level 15,000."

"Tiger 783, Tailpipe ... roger ... Neak Luong is hot with one Bird overhead ... active is runway 23 short ... traffic is Blue 46 landing, one Bird to depart ... TIA is at the ramp and will be leaving shortly ... report 20 out ... incoming is very light."

"Tiger 783 ... roger." That's good news for a change!

The thick black smoke at Neak Luong had faded and we watched the lone C-130 dump its white parachutes. The subject of accuracy came up as we all wondered how many of these chutes landed in the proper area. As they carried cargo and not people they probably fell pretty fast and the wind had been almost nonexistent. Any breeze that might have had an effect was no doubt given away by the ever-present smoke columns. A decision was reached that a high percentage of Neak Luong's supplies were going to the right people.

"Tailpipe, Tiger 783 ... 20 out."

"Tiger 783, Tailpipe ... descend and land at your discretion ... runway 23 short is active ... TIA has just left the ramp and fighters are aware of your existence." (Somehow I could tell that Tailpipe was getting a little tired of saying the same things day after day.)

"Tiger 783 ... understand ... thank you."

During our descending circles we saw TIA depart for U Tapao and were struck again by the apparent peacefulness of the scene. It was kind of like looking at a calm lake in a beautiful setting but knowing that it was full of piranhas. No puffs of smoke in the city so the only obvious signs of what was really going on were a couple of half-sunk ships and the remains of a bridge that once crossed the river.

Our arrival at the ramp was highlighted by smiles and Tiger caps. The Old Couple were busy picking up shrapnel but stopped to wave. They weren't wearing our hats. The Cambodian boss explained they didn't like the feel of them but assured us they were keeping the hats as a valued part of their meager belongings.

Big John came aboard and after he thanked us for bringing their lunch and saying how good it was, asked what he owed for it. Jim said it was on the house. And, anyway, we hadn't the slightest idea of what it cost. John began a protest but I cut him off by mentioning Ban Me Thuot. He hadn't heard anything. When I finished telling him he responded with: "Those guys that we heard on the radio yesterday morning? Holy Jesus, we were listening to them die? For God's sake, how could that happen? We heard them, didn't anyone else?"

He stared at me as if I must know something but all he got was a shake of my head and a shrug. I couldn't even begin to guess what had taken place. Having his own war, I wondered why he was so concerned about South Vietnam. Then it seemed kind of obvious.

Big John had been hoping for some kind of intervention in Cambodia, and when a major city in South Vietnam was overrun without a peep from anyone else? The handwriting on the wall was loud and clear.

You could almost see the spirit flow out of him, and like special effects in a movie he aged while he stood there. All the work, the hot days, the discomfort, and risk were now just silly things that probably, in the end, would mean nothing. As John quietly left I wondered if we were going to create some widows while chasing what was looking more and more like a hopeless cause.

Sure we got paid, but we would also get paid for flying a load of toys from Hong Kong to Seattle or a bunch of tourists from New York to St. Maarten. I think, to our credit, neither Big John nor any of us ever seriously considered turning our backs on these people in spite of the doubts and the probable outcome. Where there is a grain of hope there is ... hope.

As we started up the runway to the departure end, one lone rocket banged harmlessly into a wide-open field off to our right (southeast). What bothered us was we had never before seen one hit in that area and it could mean the Khmer Rouge were changing positions, probably moving closer. This day had given us way more than enough to think about.

Departure was problem free and as everyone felt somewhat subdued, not much was said as we drifted through our "zone of peace" at 16,000 feet above the earth. Lord Jim was transferring data into the logbook, Greg was sitting in a jump seat with his eyes closed, and Bob and I mostly just took in the view from our "window seats." As we passed a waypoint called "Echo" and turned direct for Saigon, our reverie was broken by: "Tiger 783, Saigon center ... traffic three miles ... 12 o'clock (straight ahead) ... opposite direction at 15,000 ... when clear of traffic you are cleared to descend and maintain 12,000 your discretion." I acknowledged that and watched a Boeing 727 swiftly float past beneath us, probably on his way to Bangkok and "my" seafood dinner. A few minutes later Bob started us down and I radioed: "Saigon center, Tiger 783 ... leaving 16,000 for 12." Beginning the end of our workday.

Thankfully, everything stayed "uninteresting" except for the word that Ernie Miranda's daily shipment of SM Oil had arrived and our share was waiting for us at the office. If the Food and Drug Administration had known how much we appreciated this stuff they would have pulled it off the market for testing. It was tasty, wet, cold, and one our few fragile ties to the "good old days."

We noticed a man standing in the background, late fiftyish with gray hair and wire-rimmed glasses, that had to be someone's grandfather. Lord Jim recognized him as the World Airways flight engineer (Second Officer) and motioned for him to join us. Refusing a beer, he asked Jim if they could go somewhere and talk. As they went into one of the side offices Bob and I agreed that the guy didn't look right. He was very pale and wore an odd expression. Later we came up with fear and resignation mixed. They came back just as our ride to the hotel was ready so we asked the man from World if we could give him a lift somewhere (he and his crew were staying at another hotel) but he said no thanks. He had a taxi waiting.

After we bailed into the van and got underway Jim told Bob and me an amazing little story. This World crew member (I don't recall his name so I'll use Mr. W.) was first told that he would be working a flight from Oakland (CA) to Saigon and then return home. Once here, Mr. W. was told to stay and work the Phnom Penh flights, and he did try. He was the Second Officer on the flight when they took that bad hit. After that, he asked to be replaced as he had not volunteered and wanted no more to do with this war stuff. In spite of having plenty of time while their airplane was being repaired, his request was ignored and now he was becoming physically ill, barely able to eat or sleep. Could Jim help him somehow?

Jim told him to simply refuse to fly but Mr. W. said he would be fired for doing that. Jim then pointed out the fact that, under the rules of this operation, everybody involved had to be a volunteer, period. Mr. W. said he had mentioned that to his people and their answer was that he would be fired immediately if he tried to "pull that one"!

Not Lord Jim or Bob or I could come up with anything to help this guy if he was too shy to help himself. We felt really fortunate to be flying for an outfit like ours. Our boss, Bob Prescott, or any other Tiger would never even think of forcing someone to put their life on the line, rules or no rules! I suggested maybe Mr. W. was approaching some sort of retirement thing and his "leaders" were hoping he would quit.

Kaleidoscope ... the tube was filled with blue Renault taxis, pedicabs, scooters, motorcycles, bicycles, and people: the daytime traffic in

Saigon. Navigating successfully through this we arrived at the hotel and were greeted by Maria.

When I saw her familiar, beautiful face I had an almost uncontrollable urge to grab and just hold her for a while. If she could have read my mind I'm sure she would have let me, but as it was, it was good that I resisted the impulse. Our relationship would have gone downhill in a hurry and I probably would have been rewarded with a swift kick in the shins.

Three papers were exchanged for three quarters and Maria asked if we wanted to go shopping tomorrow. When we told her we had to work she said: "That's not right, you know you guys don' look so good, pretty soon you gonna get sick!" she pointed at Jim's foot and said: "That still hurt?" Lord Jim told her that it was a little sore but would be okay. Three grown men with a thirteen-year-old mother and it felt … normal.

After a unanimous vote for a before-dinner nap, we split up and headed for our rooms. I stopped off at the CBS office and asked Peter Collins about Ban Me Thuot. The NVA had total control over that city and had taken Duc Lap as well. They had also cut the main escape route (Highway 21) to the coast, trapping troops and refugees.

A counterattack was being set up but the NVA had moved in a lot of men and equipment, making it clear that this was no minor skirmish. It didn't look good at all. Peter was now worrying about his wife's Vietnamese family as they lived in the vicinity of Danang and that could very well be the next area to come under attack. A CBS reporter and photographer were on their way to get as close as possible to the action, and no, Peter still hadn't heard a word from the man he had sent to Ban Me Thuot.

I continued on to my room, let myself in, and still fully clothed laid down and "died." Luckily, Bob woke up after an hour and a half and called Jim and me. If he hadn't, I probably would have found myself wide awake and hungry at 2 AM with nothing to do but count artillery shots until the 5 AM wake up. A quick shower later, we all met in the lobby and decided to have a light meal at our little place around the corner. I put away a nice serving of french onion soup with a salad and the usual baguette. A small glass of red wine went well with this and we finished everything off with cups of dark coffee. Even the worst days have good parts.

After the meal, we all quickly faded and headed back to the hotel for a sound sleep. The last thing I remembered was wondering where Hiram hung out when he wasn't here.

12 March 1975

South Vietnam: There were few survivors of Ban Me Thuot to spread the word about what had happened. From a woman, who with her sister and their five children were attempting to flee the nightmare: "We picked up what we could carry and ran. We closed our eyes. We did not want to open them. There were bodies everywhere and shells flying. We managed to get on a crowded bus that was going to Phuoc An but the NVA had set up a block in the road. Two North Vietnamese came to the bus and threw grenades through the windows. The bus blew up." She and two of the children survived and though deafened and suffering minor injuries, they walked the rest of the way to Phuoc An, a distance of 12 miles.

Wednesday morning. While my body parts argued with each other about getting up, I mentally figured how many days we (Jim and I) had been here. Ten? It seemed like 90. If time flies when you're having fun it sure comes to a screeching halt when you're not.

At least Hiram was on his pipe when I went into the bathroom. It would have been nice if he'd had a tail like a dog so I could tell if he was glad to see me.

After my hot shower I felt a bit better and was soon on my way down the stairs to the lobby. We crawled into the van and I told Jim I hoped he felt better than he looked. If not, we could just drop him off at the nearest undertaker. After he thanked me for the compliment I mentioned this was about the worst I had ever felt without having a hangover or the flu. We can't even rationalize being in such a bad way by lying to each other about how much fun we had last night.

At the airport, Grant told us that a new load of tires had come in. After the World Captain agreed to at least look into our techniques and some apologies were muttered, World was back in business. Grant came up with a wry smile when I said that he should at least give them a volume discount. He said he didn't mind selling tires but didn't want to come up short when it came to his own airplanes.

Our fuel and rice were up to the proper levels so the doors were closed, checklists completed, and we were on our way, unfortunately not to San Jose. We were delayed on the runway for about 15 minutes while several military helicopters, apparently carrying VIPs, flew low over the airport and came to rest near the terminal.

One could almost feel the change of atmosphere now that the North had made its first big move since South Vietnam's allies had packed up and gone home. Instead of the occasional olive-drab helicopter or C-130 passing by, there was now a constant ominous hum of war machinery that reminded you of a hornet's nest shortly after its being disturbed! That was the bad news. The good news, for us anyway, was most of this action was taking place to the northeast. This was well away from our track to and from Phnom Penh and we didn't have to be too concerned about staying out of the way.

Saigon tower finally cleared us for immediate takeoff, I acknowledged, Bob called for max power, and we were quickly back in Tiger 783's element. After the circles for altitude we headed for Phnom Penh to play another game of Rouge rocket roulette.

"Tailpipe Bravo, Tiger 783 ... level 15,000 ... 40 out."

"Tiger 783, Tailpipe ... roger ... Neak Luong is hot with one Bird overhead ... our active is runway 5 ... traffic is Blue 46 departing, TIA at the ramp, one Bird in the pattern and fighters have been notified ... call 20 out."

"Tiger 783 ... roger."

Using runway 05 we'll have a chance to check on the West End Kids as we'll be starting our takeoff from their back yard. We hope that there's not a noticeable dent in their numbers. I keep forgetting to ask Big John who these kids belong to and what their history is, if any. All of us are wary of becoming attached and maybe we don't want to know. If this situation ends as we are afraid it will, it's going to hurt like hell, even without adding the kids to our list of friends!

"Tailpipe, Tiger 783 ... 20 out."

"Tiger 783, Tailpipe ... cleared to descend and land your discretion ... active is 05 ... TIA is departing ... no other significant traffic."

"Tailpipe, Tiger 783 ... understand cleared to land our discretion ... thank you."

As downtown Phnom Penh came into view we saw at least six simultaneous eruptions of black smoke within the city and some more along the waterfront. After a bit of calculating in my head I announced to anyone listening that, if we were landing on runway 23, the falling rockets would miss us by a quarter mile, more or less, as we passed over the city. Bob said, "Thanks a lot" and added he hadn't even thought about that. And as there wasn't much we could do about it anyway, he wished I'd kept that little tidbit to myself. Lord Jim seconded the motion and threatened to hit me with the logbook.

As we made the tight, steep turn to our final approach, another puff of black smoke appeared in the open field to the southeast followed by: "All bunnies incoming ... got it Tiger?" I "rogered" that and shortly after, we touched down.

We were in reverse and slowing when a brown cloud appeared about 200 yards ahead and on the centerline of the runway! Obviously, this was the least appreciated of all the incoming ... the 105mm artillery! First the brown smoke then, as these rounds came in at an angle instead of almost straight down like the rockets, the shrapnel would also fly off at an angle away from the point of impact (to our right in this case). As we passed through the smoke we didn't hear any shrapnel hit us. The third clue was the damage this thing caused when it hit the concrete runway. We felt and heard a definite thump from the nose wheel as we ran over the hole. The rockets, mainly antipersonnel, would seldom cause noticeable damage to the concrete areas.

From Tailpipe: "Tiger that was a 105! You okay?"

This was not funny but I tried by saying: "We're okay...these guys must be cross-eyed ... not even close ... piece of cake!" My damn hands were threatening to shake again (I had to get a good night's sleep!) but the distraction of reading and responding to the always mandatory checklists helped a lot. While we taxied in, Bob asked Greg to check out the nose gear for possible damage as that pothole was probably in the "New York City" category! We laughed!

Everyone at the ramp looked grim and worked rapidly as the incoming had been frequent and sometimes frighteningly accurate. Greg checked the exterior of the airplane and went into the Tailpipe bunker to report the hole in the runway. By the time he returned, the offload was complete, Lord Jim was handing out a cold can of pop to the last man out, the boss, and doors were closing. We had number one and two engines running and were taxiing out for takeoff when Lord Jim announced our total time spent on the ramp unloading 94,500 pounds of rice was under ten minutes! Later, another crew set a record (while using the "short-cut" takeoff) with 13 minutes elapsing from landing to liftoff!

When we approached the takeoff end of runway 05 we realized the kids must have seen us at our ramp as they were standing there waiting, smiles and all. I had forgotten again to ask Big John about them and blamed it on the "105" distraction. Oh well, like I thought before, maybe we really didn't want to know anyway.

It was my turn to drive again so Bob got us into position, we quickly waved and smiled back at the kids, and I called for max power while releasing the brakes. Another rapid takeoff with the quick right turn and we were on our way back to Saigon with one more "all bunnies incoming" as a going-away present. I secretly wished that, assuming I could fly the damn thing, I could borrow a fully armed fighter from the South Vietnamese and just once cause somebody else to worry about "all bunnies incoming"! That would feel sooo good!

For once there was not a single wisp of smoke above Neak Luong. We could tell where it was because of the Bird C-130 that circled above, but how strange to not see the smoke. Near where I live in Washington State there was a large paper mill that emitted steamy smoke so consistently, for so many years, that it was a landmark. When the mill shut down it took a while for the locals to get used to empty sky when they looked in that direction. I had that feeling then as I looked to the northeast.

Now that the "hornet's nest" was stirring, Saigon center had lots of traffic at whatever o'clock to report and all four of us were keeping a sharp lookout for rocks in the road. Maybe the pilots of the VNAF C-130 that we almost tangled with had told their version of that scary story to their people and everyone was being a little more cautious. With no clouds to block the view we could see Bien Hoa airbase beyond Saigon and even from a distance could see that it was busy launching F-5 fighters, A-1 fighter/bombers, and C-130s all headed northeast to support the counterattack at Ban Me Thuot. We wished them luck.

The approach and landing were fun but uneventful and we were soon telling Grant how well his airplane was running. I hated to complain, but (tongue in cheek) had to tell him that my left armrest was stiff and hard to adjust. After flipping me a mock dirty look he fished a minican of WD-40 out of one of his many pockets and handed it to me. It worked!

World must have altered their methods as they had finished one flight so far and still had all the original tires. Grant said he had even found time for a short nap this morning. This reminded us that his day started about two hours before the first departure of each day and ended, depending on what repair work was needed, some time after the last arrival. This covered all the DC-8s on his ramp, not just Tigers. He had an excellent crew of local people, some mechanics from the other outfits, and the Tiger flight mechanics to help. But Grant was in charge and like any good pit boss (which he actually was on Formula and Indy cars) personally oversaw everything.

Trip number two of this day was a little more peaceful than the first one and we had time to worry about how hot and cold Tailpipe's lunch was. We could see someone was taking us seriously now as we noticed one vanilla and one strawberry shake was in the order along with the usual chocolate. I'll never forget the wonderful smell of those burgers.

The Khmer Rouge must have been restocking their positions. Even downtown Phnom Penh was quiet as we descended and prepared for landing. I felt it odd that the quiet, in a way, was more nerve-racking than the action. As we passed low over the west end we noticed no sign of the kids. After we were down and taxiing Greg said that he thought he spotted them close to their shacks and we all shared the thought that only a hit or near miss would keep them so far from their beloved airplanes. We hoped for the near miss.

After we parked, Big John confirmed two or three rounds had landed in that area and someone would try to check on them soon. I almost said if it was a hit I didn't want to know about it but I realized how dumb that would sound and choked it back. Damn!

John thanked us for the lunch. Lord Jim passed out refreshments to the deplaning offloaders, Greg closed and checked the doors, and after the restart we were on our way again. At the west end, a few little faces peeked out from the shanties but that was it. We paused for a second to see if we could see any bodies or other evidence of casualties, but other than the lack of smiling faces nothing seemed out of the ordinary so we moved on before we drew some fire to that spot.

After liftoff just as I started my right turn we heard: "All bunnies incoming." I looked back to the right and spotted a large cloud of black smoke drifting slowly away from Sunnybrook Farm! As it must have been a truly nasty 122mm rocket I knew the gang at Tailpipe Bravo were enjoying some loud "music" with their lunch.

Climbing out, we spotted Tiger 791 on her descent into Phnom Penh and simply said "hi guys" on the radio. They answered by sending two clicks of their mike button and Bob said: "See you later." No one felt very chatty at the moment.

This return to Saigon was uneventful but the radio talk between various entities and aircraft had lost the usual aura of professional boredom. Voices now had an edge, just a tiny bit of urgency, as aircraft and their crews were winding up to destroy and save lives. We felt like helpless and impotent bystanders in our gentle DC-8 while we fantasized ourselves as warriors in olive-drab F-4 fighters or maybe a heavily armed A-1 bomber. My only direct participation so far had been to hope I had hit a communist sympathizer with a golf ball!

My "bush pilot" approach and landing were done well but the old satisfaction was no longer there ... it no longer seemed so important.

After our arrival at the Saigon ramp we were handed a directive to initial (not from Tigers, but Col. C's office or U Tapao, I don't remember which) informing us that: "We could request, but would no longer automatically receive, advisories on the conditions at Neak Luong. That city (may it rest in peace) was not on an airway so was not shown on the charts and someone may have seen the smoke and descended to take a closer look thus exposing themselves to an encounter with a Bird parachute, SAM missile, or perhaps a collision with the Bird C-130 that was dropping the parachute." (Yup ... Yup ... we might have done that ... give me a break!) "It was now assumed to be highly unlikely that a crew without at least one person on board that didn't have this information would be involved in this operation so this advisory is hereby suspended and Tailpipe Bravo can now spend more time performing their duties."

Whew! Amazing how many words have to be expended to cover everyone's butt! In a way, dropping these advisories wasn't a bad idea as we could usually see what was going on, but we also knew that no one in the whole bloody world except the 80,000 residents of Neak Luong (plus refugees) and a handful of pilots really gave a damn about what happened there and we felt ties were being snipped, one by one. We did care and quite often requested the information, or if Tailpipe had something new they would tell us without our asking. We all solemnly scribbled on the directive, thus assuming responsibility should we do something stupid!

World Airways had apparently delivered a load to Phnom Penh during the lull seeing everyone there wearing the Flying Tiger hats that we had passed out. The World people were furious and demanded we retrieve the hats as soon as possible! Flying Tigers was now guilty of using starving people to gain free advertising via the news services! This "disgusting practice" was also grossly unfair to the other carriers involved and should cease immediately! Why, even the Khmer Rouge now think that every DC-8 that goes into Phnom Penh is a Flying Tiger! Even Col. C. had to laugh at that one and the other carriers, Trans International, Airlift International, and Bird Airways all told World to "stuff it!" TIA said our "crime" was a great morale booster for some very sad people and surely World could come up with something more urgent to worry about like staying out of the way while the rest of us tried to do our job.

Still shaking our heads we headed up-country for our last round of the day.

"Tailpipe Bravo, Tiger 783 ... 40 out ... level 15,000."

"Tiger 783, Tailpipe ... roger ... runway 05 is active ... traffic is one Bird inbound and Airlift at the ramp, they both should be gone for your arrival ... fighters have been notified ... call 20 out."

"Tiger 783 ... roger."

I wondered aloud if we were still allowed to look at Neak Luong as we passed by. No one said anything as we did look, and along with a Bird overhead, we saw a new column of gray smoke forming. And I thought *we* needed a day off.

"Tailpipe, Tiger 783 ... 20 out."

"Tiger 783 ... break ... all bunnies incoming ... Tiger 783, Tailpipe ... descend and land your discretion 05 ... Bird just departed and Airlift is positioning 05."

"Tiger 783 ... understand."

"Airlift, Tailpipe ... cleared for takeoff runway 05 ... traffic is Tiger 783 reporting 20 out."

"Airlift ... understand cleared for takeoff ... got any more hats Tiger? We'll take three."

That squeezed a smile out of everyone listening. Soon we saw Airlift climbing out as we were beginning our steep descent into the arena. More puffs of black smoke formed along the city's waterfront as the break came to an end.

On final approach, we didn't have a chance to take a quick look for the kids as "all bunnies incoming" announced the arrival of two rockets on the runway ahead of us. The shooter's aim was perfect but thankfully his timing was off by about 20 seconds or so. Of course, we were relieved but still winced when we passed through the black smoke that hung above the pavement. Now we were beginning to think there might be a spotter somewhere on the airport. But even with a spotter, aiming the rockets would be "educated" guessing at best. God help us if it rained and the 105mm artillery came into the picture. With a spotter and no puff of dust to give away their location they would have time to aim and "fire for effect," at best closing the airport. At worst?

At the ramp the special hats had been put away and everyone wore the grim expression again. A few minutes went by then three things happened at once. Someone shouted and the Cambodians either got behind something or came into the airplane. Big John sprinted to the bunker entrance. And the "all bunnies incoming" was announced. We quickly unfastened our seatbelt/shoulder harnesses and sat, waiting for hearts to either restart or stop forever. If the two engines hadn't been running there would have been total silence as no one was moving or speaking.

Then ... BLAMM!, a breath-taking shock wave, and all kinds of debris falling everywhere. The airplane moved enough to spill a cup of coffee on Jim's work table and someone's pencil went rolling across the floor. More silence, then it seemed like everyone started to chatter at once as hearing returned and the word spread that neither human or machine had suffered more than a minor scratch or two.

Wide eyed, Greg came into the cockpit and said that he had crouched down under the tail when the alarm sounded. After the blast, covered with dust and ears ringing, he paced off less than a hundred feet to the smoking hole beside the tail! He still had some humor left as he told us if he made it home for the Fourth of July he was going to join the family dog under the bed.

Big John came aboard to check on everyone and told us that everybody's luck had been more than good. This rocket was the big and really bad 122mm. Its large size and a high light gray overcast sky allowed someone to spot it sooner than usual, thus the early warning. I told John to hold the warnings from now on as I'd rather die without knowing it. This got all of us started laughing (giggling?) and even the offload crew seemed almost cheerful. Is this why bungee jumping is so popular?

After we all calmed a bit, Bob went back to pee and John asked how much longer we were going to stay on this lousy job. I told him as long as he and Tailpipe Bravo kept up their end we'd do the same. He smiled and said: "That's the answer I had for you if you asked first." He was going to say more but was rudely interrupted by the usual report of "incoming" and a thump on Sunnybrook Farm.

Offload completed, we quickly taxied to the west end and after noting the kids were still shy, commenced our last takeoff of the day. At altitude, I thought about John's question. We hadn't really talked about it but we all had come to the same conclusion at about the same time. We were trapped!

If we continued to fly supplies into Phnom Penh our friends at the airport and the city's occupants might eventually die. If we (everyone in the airlift) decided discretion was the better part of valor and pulled out, the wholesale killing of thousands of men, women, and children would start within a matter of hours! The situation was that critical. A handful of civilian volunteer aviators had been unwittingly endowed with powers normally reserved for Gods and Generals!

We never did openly address this horrible truth but it weighed very heavily on our minds and souls.

When Lord Jim called in our ETA and maintenance status Gary acknowledged and mentioned the flight from Manila had not only dropped off the SM Oil, but another crew as well. We could expect to have tomorrow off. Hooray! That gave our spirits a much needed lift and we immediately began making plans for our minivacation. Sleeping in till at least noon tomorrow was high on our list along with a wee bit of spiritual intake this evening. Great!

During our descent into the Saigon area the tone of the radio chatter seemed to reflect things were not going well to the northeast. After we parked on our ramp Grant came aboard and confirmed our suspicions by telling us the counterattack had stalled well short of Ban Me Thuot and was actually being pushed back in places. This information seriously tempered our good feelings about tomorrow and smiles faded. Thanks Ernie, your SM Oil was a much appreciated highlight during a downer of a day.

At the office someone had totaled the poundage flown on our flights alone, not counting other crews or airlines. It came to 2,737,600 pounds of rice! That would have been impressive except for the depressing fact that the estimated population (including refugees) of Phnom Penh was around three million souls. In ten hard days we had managed to deliver less than a pound of rice per person, not per day but total. I went to a window with my SM Oil and stared outside while trying to swallow a huge lump of disappointment. Not much was said during the ride to the hotel.

Maria was not around when we arrived but our papers were tucked into the message boxes along with a note. Tigers had left a message that we were to get a bit of rest and then meet in the lobby at 6:30 PM. Reservations had been made at a first-class Chinese restaurant on Tu Do Street and we were to order anything we wanted, courtesy of the company.

We followed these instructions and had about the best Chinese dinner ever. Our Director of Flight Operations, Captain Oakley Smith, was the host and during dinner I mentioned naming the airplane. He thought it was a great idea and proposed a toast to "The Tiger called Nancy." It was now official and I was to start looking for paint or whatever, to get it done as soon as possible.

After dinner, everyone kind of drifted off on their own. Showing really good judgment (and the effect of a few beers), Jim and I ignored the big "F" (fatigue) and went looking for some bright lights, loud music, and high-octane booze. About two blocks from the hotel Jim grabbed my arm and pointed out a garish neon sign that we couldn't possibly ignore…. "The Bunny Club!" On the job, Lord Jim quietly attended to business but if given some time off and a drink or two he was about as predictable as a two year old at an amusement park. Just as we were entering this "club" I almost bumped into him as he suddenly stopped. I assumed he had just noticed the bunny-costumed waitress who was cheerfully welcoming us, but I was wrong. Jim took a deep breath and loudly shouted, *"All bunnies incoming!"* I bounced off the ceiling. The two other customers in the place almost dove under the table they shared, and I would have sworn the waitress's puffy white bunny-tail popped right off her pretty behind! I'm sure we were the only ones there who knew the real significance behind Jim's outburst but to loudly and suddenly shout anything in the vicinity of a war gets attention!

After wasting the next 15 minutes convincing everyone (especially the bartender) we were harmless, we each had a double Scotch, neat, with a little water on the side. It wasn't long before we both noticed the lights were too bright, the music too loud, and the Scotch was going straight to our heads. The tab was settled and we tucked our tails between our legs and retreated quietly back to the hotel.

Good night Jim, good night Peter, and good night Hiram.

13 March 1975

Cambodia: From a Khmer Republic Army (FANK) Captain in Phnom Penh: People were running back and forth every which way, afraid to stay in the same place for too long. Sometimes the shells or rockets would fall in the center of town and everybody would flee to the river bank. Then the shells would fall on the river bank and everyone would run back to the middle of town. It just went on like this like a strange bad dream.

This time, my built-in wake-up call didn't even wait for the end of curfew and the sound of traffic. My eyes came unglued at 5 AM and I felt I could use some of Grant's WD-40 to help peel my tongue from the roof of my mouth. A few beers plus one lousy drink of Scotch and now I had to go breathe on the mirror to be sure I was still among the living.

Morning toilet duties accomplished, I crawled back into bed and proceeded to toss and turn until about 10 AM when I said to hell with it and took a shower. After that and remembering to get dressed, I made my way to the lobby and managed a smile when I spotted Jim sitting in an easy chair … sound asleep! He was clean shaven and properly dressed so I figured he had tried to start the day but only made it this far. I was standing in front of him wondering how to wake him without attracting too much attention when his eyes slowly opened. He seemed to recognize me but obviously wasn't quite sure where we were. I finally said: "Let's get some coffee" and that seemed to do the trick.

The hotel coffee shop was crowded and noisy so we decided to see if our quiet little place was open yet. Even though we knew it was too early for Maria to be here, we still looked around for her. Not seeing her we went over to Tu Do Street and turning left walked down the crowded sidewalk. I sensed a presence between us and when I looked slightly to my left saw Maria keeping pace. Without breaking stride she looked up at me and said: "You wanna go shopping?" I said "Not right now" and she answered: "I didn't think so, you guys don' look good … you go drinking?" I answered: "Just a little," and she countered with: "Yeah sure, where you goin' now?" I told her and asked if she'd join us. Just after she shrugged and nodded okay, a little street salesman about eight years old came up behind us. He let us know he was selling a large brass ship's bell by vigorously ringing the damn thing! Geez … that hurt!

Maria grabbed the little guy by the arm and after leading him a short distance away gave him a stern talking to. Then, more gently, she brought him back and told us his name was (I think) Van. She said he was a friend of hers. He looked up at us with just a trace of a tear or two and said he was very sorry. Lord Jim said it was a beautiful bell and later one of us would probably buy it. He pointed at me and said: "Larry has a boat, he'll buy your bell for sure." This put a big smile on the little guy's face and after Maria said something to him he waved and took off after someone else. I never did get that bell.

Our little cafe was just opening when we arrived and I was surprised that Mom and Pop didn't seem to see anything odd about two hung-over Americans and a 13-year-old girl acting like family. Maria really wanted a cheeseburger and fries but had to settle for a simple ham and cheese sandwich. Jim had some sweet little cakes with his coffee and I tried the onion soup.

We found it hard to come up with anything to talk about except to ask Maria how she was doing in the paper business and how her family was getting along. Her family was fine and though she wasn't getting rich, selling newspapers gave her a few bucks a day. All in all, life was pretty good and she was more than a little excited that she would soon be going to a special school for veterans' children. I tried to get her to give some details on that but she quickly changed the subject.

"How long you gonna go to Phnom Penh?" she asked. I had to tell her we didn't know. That seemed to bother her as her brow wrinkled and she said she didn't understand. I asked her how long she was going to sell newspapers.

"Till I go to school," she replied. "Anyway, nobody tries to kill me so maybe I'll do it always but you better stop goin' to Phnom Penh."

After we finished our coffee, Maria walked us back to the hotel then left us as she went to pick up her newspapers.

We checked our message boxes and Jim came up with one. Someone at World wanted him to call them asap. Wondering what this was about we went to Jim's room and he called Gary at the Tiger office to see if he knew what was going on. I could only hear Jim's side of the conversation: "Aw, the poor bastard, when? Yeah ... He wants me to what?! ... Did you tell him he'd look funny with a DC-8 sticking out of his butt? ... No, I'm not going to call him back ... Thanks Gary, we'll see you later."

Jim hung up the phone and filled me in on the details. Mr. W., the World Second Officer who had talked with Jim the other day, had been taken to a hospital after passing and vomiting blood. The World agent wanted to know if Jim, having the day off, would take his place. What a sweetheart outfit! Jim was still muttering bad things as I left for my room and a snooze.

After a long and unsatisfying afternoon nap, I joined Bob and Jim in the lobby. One of the other crews had just returned to the hotel after their day of flying and excitedly told us about the ammunition dump in Phnom Penh taking a direct hit! They said you couldn't imagine the sights and sounds that were created when it happened! As they had departed shortly after the hit, they didn't know if there were any casualties but felt there were probably at least a few. How come the other side gets all the good news?

Still chattering, they split for their rooms and left us to decide where we were going to eat this evening. After a short discussion, we kept it simple and went back to the Chinese place of the night before. All three of us had large servings of spring rolls washed down with cold beer. Really good stuff and this time no one suggested we go out and pretend to be 20-year-old fighter pilots on their first leave. We just strolled back to the Caravelle to prepare for the real wake-up call tomorrow morning.

Next door to the CBS news office there was a large, vacant office space. Tonight, as I headed for my room I noticed the door was open and several people were inside talking. I peeked in and Peter Collins spotted me immediately. Ushering me inside, he introduced me to Udo Nesch, a balding German photo-journalist who had just returned from the Ban Me Thuot area, and a young lady I only remember as "Andy." As usual for me, I almost immediately forgot her last name and her first was such a tongue-twister that we just shortened it to Andy. She was a

French Canadian from Montreal, and if I recall correctly, had just grad-
uated as a journalist.

Attractive in a dark European way, she really seemed to have it all
together except for one outstanding fault. Whenever she had a few
drinks she would show off her very closed mind and lack of knowledge
by spouting some of the most cliched and ridiculous liberal statements
I had ever heard. This evening was one of those times as everyone had
a drink in hand and the talk was on the loud side (they soon picked up
the term "debriefing" from us). Udo firmly shook my hand and clasped
my shoulder but Andy just looked at me over her drink and said what
a displeasure it was to be face-to-face with a mercenary!

That really caught me by surprise. I tried to lighten things up a
bit by saying my folks used to drive one of those but she just did an
about-face and moved away. Peter apologized for her and repeated that
she was just fresh out of school. She'll learn, he said, and I responded
by suggesting he send her to Ban Me Thuot for a few days. He said he
would but she wasn't accredited yet (whatever that meant).

I said my "good nights," went to my room, and hit the sack ...
hard.

14 March 1975

The 5 AM wake up came with a tiny bit of good news this morning. The other working crew were going to be first out in Tiger 791 so we could drag our feet a little and have a leisurely breakfast. Not a big deal but a nice touch. I looked out the window and frowned at a solid gray overcast. Would this be the day for the rain that would bring on the heaviest and most accurate shelling yet at Phnom Penh? *No! Gotta be positive about this. It is not going to rain today!* That decision made, I entered Hiram's domain and enjoyed my hot shower.

I had just finished shaving when the phone hummed again. It was Gary at Tigers passing on a request. ABC News had made arrangements to ride with us at least once into Phnom Penh and back but the final permission was to come from us. Bob said it was okay with him if Jim and I didn't mind. I said sure and Gary asked that we wear the regular uniform. No problem.

We had our lazy breakfast and were driven to the office where we expected to see a typical TV crew buzzing around. Gary met us and said he hadn't heard a thing from them since last night. We all suspected they had come up with some excuse to not cover this story. We had a list with their names on it but didn't bother adding the information to the paperwork.

Jim was just leaving to do his preflight inspection of the airplane but Gary stopped him and said he had something to discuss with all of us. One of the new pilots had come up with a very kind thought. He wanted to organize an "Operation Little Vittles." Like during the Berlin Airlift, we would drop packages containing food, candy, and small toys for the West End Kids. What did we think?

I was first to answer by saying that the airports in West Berlin had been secure with fences around them. The West End Kids already approached dangerously close to us just because of their love of airplanes, add food and toys to this and we will end up killing them with kindness, literally. Who's cockeyed idea was this? Gary said names weren't important but he (and Bob and Jim) agreed totally with what I said. He would spread the word and asked us to do the same. It was a shame we couldn't do something like this but just one little trinket would cause serious problems for the kids and us for the duration of the mission.

Time for departure arrived and we were on our way, just the usual foursome. Jim was the first to remove his uniform shirt but by the time we were at our cruising altitude we were all sporting basic Jockey white again. I mentioned that Peter Collins would donate half of his "family jewels" to make this trip but CBS had been adamant when they refused each of his several requests to do so.

"Tailpipe Bravo, Tiger 783 ... level at 15 ... 40 out."

"Tiger 783, Tailpipe ... roger ... traffic is one Bird arriving ... TIA is on the ramp to depart shortly and fighters have been notified ... call 20 out."

"Tiger 783."

Neak Luong sported one lone Bird C-130 overhead but there was an ominous lack of smoke. You would think that a good sign but somehow to us it now signified that the end was very near.

"Tailpipe Bravo, Blue 46 ... 40 out ... level 60" (six thousand feet).

"Blue 46, Tailpipe ... roger, check 20 out."

"Tailpipe, Tiger 783 ... 20 out ... we copied Blue 46 reporting 40 out."

"Tiger 783, Tailpipe ... roger ... runway 05 is in use ... traffic is TIA departing and Blue 46 ... cleared to descend and land your discretion and be advised that the city is taking a lot of bad stuff today."

"Tiger 783 ... understand."

During our circling descent we could see many black puffs in town and a few tall, white splashes in the river. The only good news was the lack of "incoming" announcements from Tailpipe. The Rouge must have been shooting all their rockets into the city. It just didn't make any sense. It might have, if surrendering was an option or if there was a strong military presence in town but neither of those conditions existed. In fact, most of the military personnel in the city were, at best, walking wounded. It was just another affirmation that Pol Pot and his cronies were not warriors but murderers. Why couldn't anyone else in this small world see that? I guessed the United Nations was merely a very large and impotent club. A place for diplomats to gather and gossip while their wives went shopping on Park Avenue.

On final approach we saw them! The West End Kids were out in force and standing right on the end of the runway while waving at us. I found myself envious of the little guys. When I was just a little one I would have been thrilled speechless to be able to stand just under a big airplane while it was landing. Lord knows I tried, but seldom succeeded. There was almost always someone (an adult) nearby who would ruin things by making certain that my life would be safe (and boring). Then I grew a bit and realized the risk of becoming roadkill was very real and would play hell with my dream of being a pilot. Now I had come full circle. Once again in harm's way, but the thrill was no longer delicious.

Landing, offload, and departure were all accomplished without a single disruption due to incoming. Even the possibility of rain was fading along with the cloud cover that bothered me earlier. This run would have been downright pleasant if we weren't wondering what Pol Pot and his weasels had in store for us next.

Flight number two was another quiet one. The overcast had thinned considerably, creating a rather colorless but very hot day. There was little wind to speak of but Tailpipe advised us runway 23 was now in use. Because of the heat and lack of incoming we decided to go easy on the brakes and roll all the way to the west end. This would also give us a chance to check on the kids.

Now what. The kids were there all right but were over 50 yards away and just quietly standing. No waves, and instead of smiles we got everything from dead-pan to outright frowns! We looked carefully but didn't see anything obvious that would indicate one of them had met with an accident. Tailpipe confirmed there had been no incoming at the west end or anywhere on the airport since our previous flight. A genuine mystery.

John came aboard and explained they were trying a new procedure. With no wind and whenever traffic permitted, they would land the DC-8s to the west, and to eliminate the long and dangerous trip to the east end for takeoff, would let us depart from the west end. What a great idea. Now we had another reason to pray for dry and calm weather. The offload went smoothly and we were soon back at the west end to start our takeoff. The kids were still standing like little mannequins just quietly staring at us as I slowly pushed up the power and released the brakes. Very quickly they were out of sight but definitely not out of mind. Puzzling ... and a bit frightening.

After lunch and an unexplained delay we once again set out for Phnom Penh. We checked in with Tailpipe at 40 miles out and by all indications things were still very quiet. I was just picking up my microphone to report 20 out when our boredom was relieved by Tailpipe reporting multiple incoming! That was the first time we'd heard the term "multiple" in a bunny report. I just started to open my mouth again when Tailpipe transmitted rapidly in the blind:

"Tiger 783 ... Tiger 783, Tailpipe ... after 20 out descend your discretion ... we'll be off (the air) for a few minutes ... stand by this frequency."

"Tailpipe, Tiger 783 ... roger."

This did not sound good at all. We had started our descent when Tailpipe got back to us:

"Tiger 783, Tailpipe ... sorry about that, they just threw a handful at us ... you're cleared to continue descent and land runway 23 your discretion ... traffic is a Bird C-130 that will be landing shortly."

"Tailpipe, Tiger 783 ... understand."

"All bunnies ... incoming."

We agreed boredom wasn't such a bad word after all. At least the city seemed quiet as we approached the Palace. I spotted the C-130 off to our left and noticed that instead of landing he was in a steep left turn. Pointing him out to Bob I said he must have gone around because of the last incoming rocket. This put him a lot closer in front of us! Bob slowed as much as he safely could and turned slightly to the right to widen our turn. As we came around with the tall TV tower now to our left we could see that it was going to be close. I was about to say something nasty about our not having compatible radio frequencies when Tailpipe read my mind: "Tiger, the Bird knows you're close and he'll keep his speed up ... he should be approaching the turnoff as you touch down."

"783 ... Thanks."

Bob was doing a great job of "chewing gum and walking at the same time," and as we lined up for our landing, the space between the two airplanes had opened enough to allow us to continue our approach. Then things kind of went to hell.

Just as the Bird C-130 touched down, a rocket (black smoke) exploded right in front of him. We could see his tail pitch up as brakes were sharply applied and the spacing we had worked so hard to gain began to disappear. All bets were called off when another hit puffed up just beside the Bird's nose and he swerved to the left raising a cloud of dust as he left the runway. Bob called for max power and as we aborted our approach the C-130 passed out of sight beneath our nose. About then, Tailpipe called and suggested we take the miss and hold somewhere. Before I could acknowledge, another "all bunnies incoming" was announced! The Khmer Rouge had apparently grown tired of wasting people in the streets of the city and switched their attention back to the airport.

We quickly clawed our way up to 12,000 feet and settled into a slow, fuel-conserving orbit over the airport area. Bob finally gave in to the overwhelming pressure of the moment and turned the airplane over to me while he composed himself, took a deep breath, wiggled his toes, and went back to pee. I used to envy the Spitfire and Hurricane pilots of the Battle of Britain, but now having had just a sample of what they experienced, the subject of my envy was reduced to the airplanes they flew, not the job they had!

Tailpipe informed us that the Bird C-130 had survived and was dropping his load on the ramp. The enemy shooters had apparently fired off all their set-ups as things had quieted considerably and we were

Offloading with a C-130 in background.

now cleared to descend and land at our discretion. Jim had already calculated our fuel situation and gave his approval for just one more attempt. Other traffic was not a problem as it had all been turned back to U Tapao or Saigon and the fighters were out sniffing around for hard targets. To this day, I wonder if we were kept around for another try because we had Tailpipe's lunch on board.

Nah! Forgive me guys for even thinking such a thing. Steve's cheeseburgers weren't that good ... were they? Besides, it wasn't just their lunch we were bringing in.

Descent, approach, and landing were all uneventful. The Bird C-130 had been delayed while its crew inspected the exterior for damage. Finding nothing serious, they restarted and prepared to return to U Tapao. They were just coming out the ramp to the runway so we rolled on past to the west end.

We began to wonder if someone had erected cardboard cut-outs as the kids were still striking the same unsmiling pose as before.

Just as we completed our right-hand u-turn I looked to my right and spotted a shirtless man about a hundred feet away staring back at me! He quickly ducked down behind a bush and I called Tailpipe. To confuse a possible eavesdropper, I said there were little kids on one side of the runway and one big one on the other. It worked. Tailpipe came right back, said they understood, and someone would come out to talk with us after we parked.

As soon as the cargo door had opened far enough, Big John squeezed through and came up to the cockpit. After I described our new friend at the west end he handed me a Colt .45 pistol. I took it just out of reflex and he asked if I knew how to use it. I said I had fired one when I was in the military, but as my instructor told me at the time, I probably couldn't hit the inside of a house with the doors closed.

I did well with other guns but the Colt .45 just didn't feel right to me. Didn't someone at Tailpipe have a nice revolver? And, wait a minute! Why are we having this little chat?

John explained how accurate and timely the incoming had been this afternoon. He and several others had come to the conclusion a spotter had set up somewhere on the airport and my sighting pretty well confirmed it. The sticky part was that this guy had chosen a heavily mined area to set up shop and the FANK people were understandably reluctant to go in after him. John said I could just open my window and pop him. I answered: "What if I miss and he decides to "pop" us? He might have a bloody AK-47 keeping him company! Why don't you have some troops go to the west end and while staying on the runway just saturate the area with grenades or whatever?"

John replied I was the only person who knew exactly which bush to shoot at and I countered with: "Ask the kids. Your Khmer Rouge spotter is probably what screwed up their attitude and I'd be willing to bet they would know exactly where he's hiding."

Bob finally got one word in with reference to the gun: "No!"

As I handed John's .45 back to him we got a partial warning: "All bunnies ... *Blamm!* A moment later ... *Blamm!* A double shock wave but no sound of shrapnel this time. The rockets hit within 50 feet of each other on the edge of the other parking spot. Where we offloaded the last time we were here! Big John thanked us for the lunch and quickly left to check for damage or casualties.

We had all four engines running and Tailpipe had cleared us to proceed to the runway when Big John motioned for us to stop. He shouted something at a FANK soldier and when he had the man's attention he pointed at the area where the rockets had landed. The soldier looked and shook his head as he ran out of sight toward the rear of the airplane. He quickly reappeared with the Old Couple in tow!

They had gone right to work on the shallow holes left by the exploding rockets. As this was just a hundred feet directly behind us they soon found themselves in the middle of a hot hurricane of kerosene-scented air when Bob added power to get rolling. Big John later told us that in spite of being on their hands and knees it was all they could do to stay in one spot! I would have guessed that the two of them together didn't weigh much more than 150 pounds.

The soldier walked them to a safe spot and grinned in our direction still shaking his head. The Old Couple just stood there, looking down like little kids that had just been caught playing doctor. She had a dark smear of thin tar down her apron and we agreed we would have Maria get a new one to bring back with us as soon as we could.

John gave us the all clear and we completed our turn to head for the runway. About halfway out the ramp Bob stopped the airplane. He said he had a hunch that our friend at the west end might be up to something. Thirty seconds passed and there it was! "All bunnies incoming," followed by a hit on the runway just west of the ramp. Followed by many undeleted expletives, sonofabitch being among the more popular.

Bob then taxied rapidly through the cloud of smoke to the west end and wondered aloud if our friend would have the balls to call one in on himself.

During the u-turn we observed the kids still in their downers and as we lined up I glared at "the bush" for a second then pushed up the power and released the brakes. Once we were on the way to our "zone of peace" and Saigon, Bob talked to Tailpipe and asked them to go easy on the Old Couple. "Lots of people have underestimated the power of jet blast or prop wash," he said. Tailpipe replied John was out checking on them now and added that just a few days ago a FANK soldier had cracked a bone in his wrist after attempting to ride his bicycle behind a powered up DC-8!

My thoughts drifted back to 1946 and a small airport near my home just outside Spokane, Washington. An Air National Guard squadron of P-51 Mustang fighters was based there and I guessed I was about the luckiest kid alive to be able to walk right up and touch these wonderful machines. On occasion, a mechanic would start one up and run tests with a fairly high power setting. I soon discovered the fun to be had by sneaking under the fence and standing behind the airplane. If you kept your balance you could assume ridiculous angles. If not, you would be blown into the fence.

Calvin and Hobbes would have loved it!

An AT-28D. Several countries, including France, flew these planes as ground-attack fighters.

This remained relatively harmless until the day I introduced a friend to the sport. When the airplane was being started we crawled under the fence. It was a very cold day, and of course, I didn't notice the sheet of ice on a puddle between the tail of the P-51 and us. For several weeks after, my friend resembled a Frankenstein project because of the row of stitches in a straight line across his forehead! While I ate supper "standing up" that evening I wondered why I was always the one to blame when something like this happened.

Bob brought me back to the present by asking how we were going to tell Maria what an apron was. I said maybe Grant would know the Vietnamese word for that but then I had a better idea. Using a blank piece of paper on my clipboard I drew a barely reasonable facsimile of a lady wearing one. I proudly showed it around to very poor reviews. Jim asked what made it a lady and I pointed out her scarf. "It looks like a little fat guy with funny hair to me," he answered. I held out the board and suggested he draw his version but he turned me down and said: "Maria's pretty smart, she'll figure it out."

We heard Tiger 791 check 40 out but the haze kept us from spotting it. Bob said: "Good afternoon" and they replied saying that the SM Oil was early today. Leave a few for them.

As we drifted toward Saigon we listened to a lot of serious-sounding radio chatter but couldn't make sense of most of it as it was one sided. Saigon center would say something to an aircraft but because it was too far away (from us) or on another frequency we couldn't hear the answer. This was cause for a lot of speculation on our part. Especially when the city of Pleiku was mentioned quite frequently. It was now common knowledge that Pleiku was probably the next item on North Vietnam's shopping list and what we were listening to seemed to confirm it.

The rest of this final flight of our day was uneventful and we soon found ourselves filing out of our wonderful, maintenance-free airplane to board Grant's van. Grant asked if anything needed attention. We did think it would be a good idea to take a close look at the tail for any shrapnel damage. We hadn't heard any hit the airplane but the closest hits were behind us. He said: "No problem," and passed that on to the Vietnamese mechanics. On the way to the office we told him about hearing Pleiku mentioned on the radio and he said that city was probably going down the tubes sometime during the next few days.

We wanted to see Maria as soon as possible so we grabbed two SM Oils a piece and headed for the hotel.

After the newspaper ritual, I showed Maria my drawing. The conversation did get a little strange but not for the reason we had worried about. As soon as I pointed to the critical part of the sketch she said: "That's an apron, my Mom got some of those." I told her that we knew it was an apron. When I paused to think of what to say next, she said: "If you know then why you ask?"

I turned to Bob and Jim but they just shrugged and stared back with smiles that said I had the ball, now run with it.

"You been drinkin'?" she asked. I said of course not, we just got off work, and told her to be quiet and listen. She stared at me and politely waited for my next words. I said: "We need an apron for a friend in Phnom Penh."

"Why he need an apron?" I should have known that was coming!

Bob had turned around and I thought I could see his shoulders jiggling a bit. I said: "*She* needs a new apron." I quickly added: "She works at the airport and she fell down and she ruined her apron because she was too close to our airplane!" It must have been stress relief, fatigue, or both setting in but once Bob started laughing he couldn't stop.

What started it was my clumsy effort to explain what should have been simple but he was afraid Maria would think it was her fractured English causing tears to run down his cheeks. He walked down the sidewalk a bit with his shoulders heaving and his back turned to us while passersby gave wide birth to this strange person. Jim was no help, either, as he was biting his lip to keep a straight face. Thanks a lot, guys. Now I had the feeling even Maria was about to start laughing.

Instead, she actually tried to help by asking what kind of apron this lady wants. I almost fell back into the hole I'd dug by saying she needs a strong one because she carries sand in it. Maria: "Why she do that?" Me: "When the bad guys shoot at us they sometimes make holes where we put our airplane and this lady puts sand in those holes."

Now she had to go and change the subject.

"Someday they gonna make holes in you an I'm gonna be sad when you guys don' come back" then (thank goodness) "I can get a good apron for her, is she pretty?"

Feeling some relief I replied: "Not as pretty as you" (instant pink cheeks!), "and she's very, very old. How much money do you need?"

She figured five dollars would cover it with change left over and called to one of her little helpers. Taking my fiver he listened carefully to her instructions and then took off down the street. After Maria said the apron and our change would be at the hotel counter in the morning, she left us for a new group of paperless hotel guests.

When he was able to control his laughter, Bob said he was too tired to take a nap before dinner. He was just going to take a quick shower, get something to eat, and go to bed early. Jim and I felt the same way so we all agreed to meet in the lobby after about 40 minutes or so. Jim and Bob went to the elevator while I headed up the stairs to my second-floor room.

I couldn't resist popping into the CBS news room for a second to get their latest on Pleiku or whatever else might be happening. Peter wasn't around at the moment but I was told that they were drafting an obituary for that city! I thanked the person and retreated to my room.

While I drained my warm two-pack of SM Oil I once again tried to make some sense of the weird stuff piling up in my head. South Vietnam is falling! The North is picking up momentum while the South is coming unglued! Years of turmoil, thousands upon thousands of lives destroyed or damaged on all sides. All these chips tossed into the pot and now only two players remain. One has skill and confidence. The other is frantically looking for the wild cards (sophisticated equipment) his friends took with them when they folded and went home.

If the communist North prevails I don't think they can say they won. If you're the last one to bleed to death does that mean you won? If asked, Maria would have answered "I don' think so." But neither she nor I were politicians so I guess we just didn't see the "big picture." Something positive should have come from all this extreme effort and sacrifice.

I stepped down from my soap box, retreated to the shower, and beat myself to life with pressurized hot water. Hiram enjoyed the steam while he sat on the toilet pipe preening himself.

Just as the three of us hit the lobby the other crew came in. They had some good news. The West End Kids were back into their usual good spirits, the incoming was almost nonexistent, and the Khmer Rouge spotter's body had been found! It was a bit of a mystery but someone had shot him cleanly through the neck. Those who live by the sword… ?

We were just too pooped to wait for the other guys so we said we'd see them later as we left for our quiet place. I don't remember what Bob and Jim ordered but I had a green salad, cream of mushroom soup, and the usual whole baguette with a disgusting amount of butter. So good!

When I returned to my room it was just dark enough to allow flashes of artillery and the soft long distance glow of flares to show. Mother Nature added a thunderstorm to the display. I was almost reluctant to mind my heavy eyelids and crawl into bed but when I did, sleep came almost instantly.

15 March 1975

South Vietnam: At exactly 1200 (noon) local time, the American embassy in Saigon issues an order stating that all American personnel are to leave Pleiku as quickly as possible. The evacuation is to be accomplished discreetly to avoid panic among the local inhabitants but many of these people are beginning to wonder. Soon suspicions are confirmed when South Vietnamese troops in and around the city start their withdrawal. What would become known as the "convoy of tears" begins with a trickle that will grow to become a sad river of humanity flowing down Route 7B to the coast.

For the rest of my life I'm going to hate 5 AM. I remembered when being awakened at this time of day often meant fishing. Salmon or trout fishing. A peaceful sunrise, quiet solitude or warm companionship, and a promise of wonderful food cooked over a woodsy bed of coals.

That picture faded as I reluctantly gained enough awareness to answer the phone. *Why did I always end these morning exchanges with: "Thank you"? Thank you for what! Hey, the guy's just doing his job, and besides, he lives here. Your problems, if your luck holds, are temporary. An adventure in a foreign land. What is he looking forward to?*

When I grumped my way into the lobby Bob was out front standing by the van and Lord Jim was retrieving the neatly wrapped apron Maria had left at the front desk. In the van and on our way, we opened the package and found a nice but sturdy apron made of a kind of soft canvas (muslin?) that had shiny stainless "D" rings for the ties. We were glad it wasn't too fancy as we doubted the Old Woman would have worn it had that been the case. She probably would have just folded it neatly and stored it away with her other meager treasures such as the Tiger baseball hat.

Maria had also included change from my fiver. It was in piasters (local currency) but she had obviously used the black market. At the official rate I almost had my five bucks back!

The morning chatter at Steve's Place had grown a lot louder and more animated since the smoldering war had rekindled. We actually had to raise our voices to be heard over the conversations of real and wannabe experts. Steve himself made a rare appearance to proclaim he was not leaving Saigon, no matter what! He had worked too hard and long to establish his small business and he was not about to just walk away from it. "Communists eat, don't they?"

Someone piped up: "Sure, but they ain't gonna pay you for it!" Another voice asked him where he was going to get the fresh eggs and meat and other stuff to serve to anyone. Steve said he'd buy it, just like he did now. But someone else spoke up, and rather bluntly, told Steve to give it up. "Stop dreaming, reserve a couple of seats on China Airlines and get the hell out!"

A loud crash and a string of expletives from the kitchen announced that something breakable had obeyed the law of gravity. Saved by the bell, Steve left the downhill conversation and went back to resume control of his "office."

No one said it out loud but we all wondered how the communists would treat Steve and his wife if they did stay. His being an American was at least two strikes against them, but his African heritage? No one seemed to know the North Vietnamese attitude toward such things. Maybe it would work in Steve's favor but we suspected the opposite was far more likely.

In a somber mood we finished our coffee, paid the bill, and headed for the airport. How many more meals would we consume at Steve's and what would become of him and his wife? Oh well, if they wanted, they at least had somewhere to go when the balloon popped. Small comfort.

We studied faces on the way to the airport and noticed smiles were now quite rare and whenever eye contact was made we felt a touch of animosity in the stares. Was it real or just our imagination? A feeling of guilt on our part? Maybe a bit of everything.

The weather this morning kind of matched our mood. Because of a high gray overcast everything looked colorless and even cold if we ignored the 80° temperature. Of course, this made us think of the dreaded rain that would come sooner or later allowing the Khmer Rouge to really dump their stuff on Phnom Penh. What an "interesting" life we had slipped into.

On arrival at the Tiger office we found out the day's schedule had gone to hell in the last 20 minutes! Sudden accurate and heavy incoming had forced TIA's DC-8 to abort their landing at Phnom Penh and they were now circling overhead the airport. They would have to make a decision based on their fuel situation sometime in the next 20 minutes.

Word came in they were descending for another approach. After a few minutes another message came saying the second attempt had been scrubbed and TIA was now returning to their base at U Tapao, Thailand.

Next in line, the World crew on the ramp next to us in Saigon started up and were soon on their way. We were to be next but it was decided we would wait until World was on the ground in Phnom Penh. By the time that was confirmed, TIA was back in position for another try. Nap time!

Finally, after about four hours or so we had Tailpipe's hot lunch on board and were cleared to start. We'd be doing well to fly two trips today ... not good.

Saigon cleared us to proceed to runway 25 Left and we smiled a little as Grant briskly ushered us onto the taxiway and finished with a smart salute. If our job could have been made any easier or safer it certainly wasn't Grant's fault.

On the runway we patiently waited while the control tower set up a gap in the flow of VNAF helicopters for us to squeeze through. We had the power up a bit with the brakes locked ready for the quick go. When the word came ... we went! This really would have generated passenger complaints if we'd had any aboard.

We were quickly above the majority of traffic and we all relaxed ever so slightly as we settled into the routine of transporting zillions of tiny white grains of rice. Not to a wedding, but to a place where they were literally worth life itself.

Crap! I had tuned in Tailpipe just in time to hear "All bunnies ... incoming!"

"Tailpipe, Tiger 783 ... 40 out ... level at 15,000."

"Tiger 783, Tailpipe ... continue inbound ... report 20 out ... one Bird will be departing shortly."

"Tiger 783 ... understand."

You could feel a change in the air. Electricity? Yes, but the "crackle" had been replaced by a low, ominous hum. The sun was visible in the haze above us but somehow it seemed dark. Maybe when we get a good night's sleep everything will seem a little better. Once again I thought about what it would feel like to live here with no way out. Choices limited to: pain, more pain, or death!

Good ... you've got something to do, it's almost time to call Tailpipe. If you're not going to get out of here, stop thinking so much!

"Tailpipe, Tiger 783 ... 20 out."

"783, Tailpipe ... descend your discretion ... plan on runway 23 ... no significant traffic."

"783 ... understand."

As we settled into our steep spiral descent we could see lots of hits in the downtown area and a few in the river. One of us came up with the idea of running some well-protected barges up the Mekong River and evacuating these poor souls. A realist in the group pointed out panic would be a deterring factor. The barges would be swamped within minutes of their arrival! There were just too many people, and without strong outside help, no options.

When we were in the final left turn for our approach, a fighter appeared low and to the north. Trailing a thin stream of grayish smoke he was obviously in trouble and headed straight for the airport. I reported this to Tailpipe and they replied by saying they did not have radio contact with him and apparently he was too low for visual contact. Would we keep track of him? I affirmed that and told Tailpipe we would slow as much as possible and he should end up well ahead of us. I added we would be well prepared to abort our landing if necessary. Tailpipe thanked us and advised they now had the fighter in sight.

We watched as the entire Pochentong (Phnom Penh) Airport fire department (one lone LaFrance crash truck) moved into position beside the runway.

Our little friend landed okay with plenty of room for us behind but he had a problem. His speed after touchdown left no doubt that his brakes were not working! We were on our short final approach when the pilot of the fighter eased his airplane off the right side of the runway. When in the soft dirt he came to a safe stop, creating a cloud of dust. This left us plenty of room, and when it was learned the pilot was uninjured, everyone was happy.

At the ramp we noticed an oil-streaked gray UH-1 (Huey) helicopter parked off to the side and two Air America pilots talking to Big

John. John pointed at us and then motioned to be sure he had our attention. Bob opened his side window and held his hand to his ear. The Air America Captain (they wore light gray jump suits with striped epaulets denoting rank) pointed at himself then toward Saigon and then at us. It was obvious they wanted a ride to Saigon and Bob didn't hesitate to nod and give them a circled thumb and finger okay sign. They each grabbed a small kit bag and came out to board our airplane.

There wasn't time for more than a few quick words before Phnom Penh had its rice, the Tailpipe crew their lunch (with the Old Woman's apron tucked into the box), and we were reading checklists. Safely airborne and on our way, we finally had a chance to chat with our surprise passengers.

They had been flying in and around Phnom Penh trying to help in any way they could. Mainly they were either transporting MDs between aid stations or bringing wounded (mostly civilians) to these stations. Twice in the last few days they had been approached by armed FANK military people who demanded to be taken somewhere. Each time, after they explaining they only had a few minutes of fuel left (which was usually true), the would-be hijackers apologized and left the scene.

Their chopper finally took one hit too many and they were barely able to make it to the airport before the last of the oil leaked out and the poor machine quit altogether. Were they headed for a little rest and relaxation in Saigon? No, they were on their way to get a another helicopter and return to Phnom Penh before dark! There was just too damn much to do.

Next came our least favorite question: "Any word of intervention? Was some kind of help on the way?" Bob got busy on the radio and I shuffled paperwork while changing the heading about half a degree. They looked at Lord Jim, and I heard a loud "shit!" after Jim shook his head. I looked back upon hearing that and noticed the Air America Captain, who was sitting in the forward jump seat (just behind Bob), had turned to stare outside while his face reddened and his jaw muscles worked. I knew these guys had seen and done just about everything during their careers with Air America but I thought I saw a trace of tears well up in the eyes of this obviously frustrated gentleman. I thought about this exclusive "club" that we all had somehow joined.

After a few minutes had passed he asked why World Airways seemed to have a rod up their butt. He and his co-pilot had asked them about a ride to Saigon and the answer was: "We'd be glad to but it's

strictly against regulations ... insurance and liability, you know." (!!??)
TIA would have taken them to U Tapao but there was no Air America operation there. Or, they could just cool their heels while Air America pulled another crew off the line to come and get them. Big John
told them we'd be there soon and he was sure they would have their
ride. We explained how World seemed to be owned and staffed by aliens
and how we sometimes suspected they were not on the same side as the
rest of us.

Maybe we could advise the Khmer Rouge what they were doing
was "against regulations." We'll put that in writing and have someone
from World deliver it to Pol Pot in person.

We were blessed with an uneventful arrival at Saigon and before
we could finish our "see ya laters" to our new friends the reload had commenced. I think they were impressed. Tiger Operations had passed on
our passenger list to Air America and a car was waiting. After hearty
handshakes and sincere "good lucks" we watched them drive away.

We told Grant he'd be out of a job if all his airplanes ran as well
as ours. He smiled and left to see if someone around here needed his
services. Jim let us know that he'd made up a special tool kit for Tiger
783. He held up a pencil and a pair of pliers wrapped in a shop rag.
This gave our smile muscles some rare exercise.

The run back to Phnom Penh was also uneventful. Even the city
was getting a breather but nobody expected it to last long. Parked and
with offload started we had a chance to look around. There she was!
The Old Woman stood off to the right and when she saw she had our
attention she stroked her new apron and beamed a smile so wide you'd
think it was a dress from Saks! The Old Man was about ten feet behind
her and he also had a smile and a wave for us. I don't think I've ever
felt so generous and warm over such a small gift.

In spite of the noise I opened my side window and gave a hearty
thumbs up. Smiling and waving, Bob and Lord Jim showed their
approval. When she saw our three ugly faces beaming back at her she
got a little shy and looked away. The Old Man shook his head a little
and still smiling pointed at his eye while he looked at us. We understood.

Even the Khmer Rouge cooperated during our little party as we
didn't hear a single warning for "all bunnies."

Without the usual interruptions we were moving again in no time.
A quick run down to the west end, a wave and smile for the kids, and
we were on our way back to Saigon for what would be our last run of

this day. I wondered aloud about how to impress Maria with the importance of what she had done. We all agreed that we'd try but being 13 years old, she probably wouldn't care too much about stuff like that.

Even open combat settles into a routine of sorts. Getting in and out of Saigon was becoming easier and, no doubt, safer as the initial panic was replaced by quiet desperation. We slipped on down, landed, and parked with minimum effort. Grant gave us a ride to the office where the cold SM Oil awaited and we stood around wondering if we'd forgotten something. This day had ended too smoothly. For us, anyway.

Our van negotiated the Saturday afternoon traffic okay and soon deposited us in front of the hotel. We were just a little early and Maria hadn't arrived yet. Although not much had been accomplished today we felt tired as usual and opted for a before-dinner nap. Bob volunteered to make certain we were all properly harassed until we met in the lobby around 5 PM. On the way to my room I came to the CBS office and noting they seemed quite busy just continued on my way.

My head made a comfortable dent in the pillow, my eyes closed, and ... the phone hummed! I was preparing to be a bit rude to whoever dared to intrude on my little coma when I noticed two things. It was darkening outside and it was Bob's voice repeating "hello" on the phone! I was confused but I found my tongue and answered. He said he had overslept a bit and it was now 5:30 PM. Wow! That wasn't a bed in my room, it was a time machine. After I convinced him I was fully awake he said he'd see me downstairs after a bit and how about Chinese food tonight? My mind was still flopping around but I just said: "Sure, great!"

It was great! A double serving of crispy, tender spring rolls accompanied by a subtle sweet and sour sauce and a couple of icy Tiger beers to wash it down. A pot of tea and some delicate almond cookies later, I almost felt human.

As we made our way back to the Caravelle we took in the sights and sounds of a Saturday evening in Saigon. One sight never failed to amaze me. Motorcycles twisting tightly through traffic with Dad driving and Mom plus one or two kids sitting behind. All quite relaxed and happy with the arrangement. Doesn't everyone do it this way? I'm sure it happened now and then but I never saw even a minor accident.

We missed Maria. She wasn't around when we left for dinner and when we returned we found our newspapers waiting for us at the front desk. The question of the moment was, how to kill an hour before bedtime. The problem was solved when a couple of Peter Collins' people stopped to say hello. After I introduced them to Bob and Jim they said a staff meeting had just turned into a debriefing and we should come on up. We had to fly again tomorrow (no booze) but this sounded interesting. We fell in and followed them up the stairs.

I spotted Udo Nesch and introduced everyone. He had just returned from a small town called Phuoc An, about 20 miles southeast of Ban Me Thuot, and had told us about a woman he had interviewed there. She had barely escaped from Ban Me Thuot only to be riding in a bus that was blown up by communist forces. She and two children survived. Hiding during the day and walking at night they covered the remaining 12 miles to Phuoc An.

While Udo was talking I noticed Andy had quietly joined our group. As soon as she could, she started a "cross-examination" by asking Udo if he had proof that communists were responsible for this woman's plight. Couldn't they have been South Vietnamese men in disguise? Udo put on a sad-angry expression, excused himself (to us), and walked away. Andy was turning away when I asked her if she had a personal problem or were all French Canadians so terribly rude!?

I heard a small voice in my head say "All bunnies … incoming" as she spun back to face me.

"Rude?" she responded. "Is not making a profit by interfering with a civil war, rude? This political re-adjustment would be settled by now if you Americans had minded your own business!"

Now I was getting a bit steamed. "Cold-blooded murder," I countered, "is a political re-adjustment? Who the hell wrote your dictionary lady? Adolf Hitler or Josef Stalin?"

She replied: "I feel sorry for poor Udo but I see your CIA has you thinking the same thoughts."

As she took in the very angry expressions on all our faces she seemed to soften a bit and with a thin sympathetic smile apologized for calling me a mercenary.

"I think you really believe the bullshit they're feeding you" added Andy as she again turned away.

I quickly conferred with Bob about taking on a passenger. He said okay but it would be my responsibility. I reminded him he was the Captain and he said he wouldn't notice his First Officer had smuggled a someone on board … until it was too late. That sounded pretty thin but I took it.

Nearing Andy, I thought about why it was so important to try to turn her around. I guess she seemed an outstanding example of the left-sided garbage being fed to the student generation of the day and I just knew if she could get a peek at the real thing it may change something.

She noticed my approach, and turning to face me, said: "I think we've talked enough for one evening."

I ignored that and took her off to the side.

"Why," I asked, "don't you go to Phnom Penh and see the situation for yourself?"

She replied: "I'd love to but the CIA wouldn't allow it. He denies it, but I know they are stopping Peter from going. They also stopped ABC News."

I asked if that's what ABC told her.

"I haven't talked to them but why else would they not go?" she said.

I muttered something about cold feet and when she asked what I said I answered: "Never mind. Can you speak French?"

"Of course," she answered, "you know where I'm from. Why do you ask?"

I said I was sure she didn't know any Cambodian but French would get her by.

I told her she was free after the fact to say anything she wanted, but until then, to keep secret what I was about to say. She was to meet us in the lobby at 6 AM sharp. Wear walking shoes, jeans, and the most masculine short-sleeve shirt or blouse she had. Have her Canadian passport and any press ID she had on her person but no cameras. If she followed these conditions exactly, we would take her to Phnom Penh in the morning.

She accepted the challenge by saying: "I'll be there!"

I said: "You'd better be or no one will even try to listen to you again."

I had the feeling she was serious when she set aside a fresh drink, said good night to all, and left for her room. Bob came up to me and wondered aloud where we should begin our search for new jobs. If something went wrong not even Tigers would eat this one.

Hiram was nowhere to be seen when I got "home" but there were some flares, flashes, and "bumps" outside. It all seemed a bit closer than usual.

16 March 1975

I was awake when the wake-up call came. I had fussed all night over the "Andy" situation and never did feel really comfortable about what we were going to do.

Added to the flashes and thumps was a new bit of action to bother light sleepers. An AC-119 gunship circled Saigon most of the night. The AC-119 was a basic cargo workhorse converted to a mean junkyard dog. Equipped with the latest in night-vision and infrared detection equipment it had a brace of rapid-fire "Gatling" guns poking out the left side of the fuselage. Rapid-fire in this case meant 6,000 rounds per minute per gun! Anything warm or visible moving around in certain clear zones during the night would be a potential receiver of this mass of missiles.

As the gunship came and went all night, the engine noise wasn't that bad but knowing the tremendous roar these guns make when fired keeps you from totally relaxing while you sleep with one ear open. I don't remember this airplane ever shooting at anything but the potential was always there. After a while I kind of became accustomed to it and found more worrisome things to lose sleep over.

After the wake-up call I went into the bathroom and nodded "good morning" to Hiram as he looked forward to my shower steam to preen by. I felt lucky. Most folks would need expensive and dangerous drugs to have a crazy morning scene like this.

I left the stairs and Bob and Jim came out of the elevator at the same time, 10 minutes to 6. Just a few minutes later the elevator came to life and returned to discharge Andy. Seeing the looks on our faces she looked down at her blouse. A bright blue with a flower embroidered above the left breast ... blouse.

"It's the best I could do," she apologized. As the smallest member of our crew, Jim silently volunteered by ushering Andy back into the elevator. After a few more minutes they returned and Andy was wearing a short-sleeve light blue uniform shirt over a white tee shirt. Much better! Our first possible obstacle, the MP just outside the hotel, barely glanced at the four of us as we climbed into the van, then went back to his cigarette and bored vigilance.

To get Andy on the airport before it became too light out we passed on the traditional breakfast in favor of rolls and coffee on the airplane. The van dropped Bob and I at the office, then took Andy and Jim directly to Tiger 783. Our proposed schedule today was interesting as we were going to do four trips as quickly as we could. I didn't know then why it was set up that way, but this was good. It meant Andy would be on the ground at Phnom Penh for the shortest possible time.

When we arrived at the airplane Grant didn't say a word about our passenger as he briefed us on tire conditions and other items but when he finished gave us a raised eyebrow grin.

Bob just said: "We'll explain later."

As Bob stowed his kit and adjusted his seat I gave Greg a quick and dirty explanation and he whispered: "You guys are frigging crazy!" I said I'd tell him more later and he went back down the boarding stairs shaking his head.

We nibbled on rolls and sipped coffee while Jim familiarized Andy with our "office" and its furnishings. Greg seemed to accept her presence as he looked for and found a fairly clean and small flak jacket for her. She was still surprisingly cool and displayed an intelligent curiosity. She said she had never been in the front end of a large airplane before and Bob told her the biggest difference between us and passengers is: "We are the first ones at the scene of the accident." *Hey ... she smiled!*

Time to depart finally arrived and we went through the familiar routines. Greg graciously offered "his" jump seat (behind Bob and with the best view outside) to Andy and got her buckled in.

Our moment of truth. Saigon tower cleared us for takeoff, I acknowledged, and Bob called for max power. Not being even close to our maximum takeoff weight of 355,000 pounds (a lot of which would have been fuel on longer flights) we accelerated smartly and as Bob smoothly raised the nose for liftoff there was a loud, appreciative "Wow!" from Andy. As soon as I could, I glanced back and saw sparkling eyes above pink cheeks and a huge grin. She was a good looking lady!

Wait a minute! Where's the pain-in-the-ass pinko ice princess? Doesn't she have the foggiest notion where she's headed? Of course not! Because of her "charming personality" no one was anxious to share experiences with her and what she did overhear, she didn't believe!

Now I was beginning to have real misgivings about this dumb thing we were doing. I thought about it for a bit and reminded myself if the stuff was hitting the fan, we would abort. Or if we got down, Andy would remain on board and we'd simply bring her right back to Saigon. If things were quiet enough to leave her, we'd be back to get her in about an hour and a half. The guys at Tailpipe will take good care of her. I guessed it would work out okay.

We pointed out Neak Luong with the usual Bird C-130 overhead. After watching it eject some parachutes Andy said this seemed like a lot of trouble, "Why don't they just surrender?" she asked.

Bob said they would do so in a heartbeat if it were a choice, but all they could do at the moment was to try and stay alive until some sort of miracle (intervention) took place.

Andy then said: "It doesn't make sense. If the military would get out of town the common people could get on with their lives."

That's when I stepped in and said: "What doesn't make sense is the fact there are only enough military personnel left in Neak Luong to keep a takeover by the Khmer Rouge from being easy. The Rouge are just waiting for the opposition to wither on the vine. Once they do move in, every man, woman, and imperfect child will be slaughtered." She started to say something but I continued. "Pol Pot's big thing is to virtually eliminate any Cambodian who has been contaminated by western influence or education. Even wearing glasses puts you on death row! He makes other so-called Communist leaders look like little league coaches!"

"But why would this be true?" she said.

I answered with a question: "Why would anyone ever make up such a grotesque story? It took a while before we believed it and now it seems the rest of the world isn't going to join us until it's too late."

It was hard for us to believe but she had no counter attack. She just sat back in the seat and nibbled her lower lip while staring outside. Jim smiled at me and winked, Bob quietly stared ahead, and I called Tailpipe with 40 miles out.

"Tiger 783 this is Tailpipe ... roger ... traffic is TIA to depart shortly and one Bird arriving ... incoming spotty but downtown is catching a few ... expect runway 23 ... call 20 out."

"Tiger 783 ... understand ... Please have John come aboard as soon as possible ... OK?

"783, Tailpipe ... will do."

Things remained quiet at the airport and as we parked I thought: *"Good luck Andy"* as I mentally crossed my fingers.

John came into the cockpit, and after introductions were made, was really glad that Andy, a reporter, had come to help spread the word. No one felt it necessary to point out the fact she was a rank beginner. Actually, just doing what she was doing today put her way ahead of some of the pros we had met. She certainly had enough "balls" to make up for at least some of her lack of experience.

Andy shook each of our hands, gave us a weak grin, and followed Big John. You could tell she was finally getting a little nervous. They came into view as John led her toward the Tailpipe bunker and she turned once to wave at us.

Greg reported "doors closed and checked," engines were restarted, and we went to the west end to wave at the kids. Bob squared us away and I pushed up the power. I had just rolled level from the right turn when Bob announced he saw three hits in the downtown area. I'm sure all our thoughts were the same. *"Please Mr. Pot, stay away from the airport for a while."*

I said maybe we should have just brought her back but good ol' "cool man" Bob just said: "Nah, she'll be okay. If we hadn't taken her and she got hit by a bus, how would you feel? John'll take care of her."

Greg said: "What if we get clobbered and can't bring her back?"

Bob looked at him for a moment and said: "Well, I guess I'd just roll over in my grave if that happened."

Lord Jim piped up and said: "I kinda like her."

Back in Saigon we told Grant the full story and he said he'd make sure she got safely off the airport and into a cab. Everything was falling into place and I was beginning to feel better about our little caper. We all agreed she seemed to be learning something already and won't Peter Collins be surprised when we bring him back a real journalist in place of the intern we "borrowed."

Everything was running like clockwork and we were soon on our way back to Phnom Penh. Surprise ... apparently there was something left to burn in Neak Luong! As we passed that area, we saw a lazy column of rich black smoke rising several thousand feet into the air. When I contacted Tailpipe I asked if there was anything new going on at "November Lima." The answer was negative.

We were relieved to hear everything was still quiet at the airport though the city was still taking an occasional hit. High anxiety was our only problem as we all looked forward to seeing Andy and hearing what she had to say. I was tempted to ask Tailpipe about her but I was afraid of sounding like a clucking mother hen. I did ask about the "incoming" situation and Tailpipe answered with a well-coded phrase: "We're still waiting for the first shoe to drop." Knowing the "shoe" would drop anytime now, we felt our adrenaline pumps start turning. When you know something is coming, silence can be very unnerving. Other than checklists and other official chatter (speeds, etc.) nothing was said as we lined up to land on runway 23.

Big John was waiting on the ramp but Andy was nowhere in sight. We assumed she was probably still inside Tailpipe saying "adieu" to new friends.

John came into the cockpit and said: "She's gone!" Eight eyeballs instantly locked onto him! "She got on a frapping rice truck and went into the city! I would've said something to the truck guards but I had no idea she'd pull this. Did you know?"

Bob said: "Hell no!"

I couldn't talk so I just shook my head.

John said he had spread the word for all the drivers and the three or four guards on each truck to watch for her as they made their runs. She had shown her press ID to the Lieutenant in charge of one of the trucks and the last anyone saw of her she was sitting between him and the driver as they left for the city. John wasn't really sure just where she was until that truck returned (without Andy) and the officer told him. Unfortunately, a rocket had exploded in the street ahead of them wounding several people and killing two. To make things even worse, a guard had to drag one bloody body to the side so the truck could pass without running over it. After that, you'd think anyone in their right mind would have stayed with the truck and come right back to the airport but not our Andy! I felt sick.

Big John said someone would find her and not to worry. Sure! At least this took our minds off the upcoming incoming. The offload went smoothly and we launched again for Saigon.

Could Jim and I find someone to sit in for us while we went to Phnom Penh (city) and searched for Andy? If we did, it wouldn't be long before everyone would know what we had done. Besides, none of us had ever set foot in that city and we probably would end up more lost than she was. Speaking French was an advantage she had that we didn't. We decided to do the only thing we could do … just sit on it for a while.

Back in Saigon, Grant's only reaction after we told him what had happened was to slide his finger across his neck while staring at us. He said: "That's great, guys. I knew about it. Greg and John knew about it. A lot more than three heads are going to roll if your lady runs into trouble."

He also reminded us she was in a foreign country without the blessing of customs or immigration. Even though a war was going on, there were probably a few bureaucrats left who were stupid enough to worry about such things. Then there's the military. I weakly pointed out that a FANK Lieutenant had taken her off the airport.

Grant slam dunked that by pointing out the fact Lieutenants don't count when it comes to a situation like this. Some senior officer with a hair to split might really make a scene just to divert attention from his Rouge problems!

"Good luck," he said as he left the cockpit.

The tall, congenial, skinny mechanic had just shredded our shorts and we (I?) probably deserved it! Greg started to wonder out loud about his job but Bob cut him off by saying he was the goddam Captain and Greg hadn't had any choice but to go along for the ride.

Things stayed fairly quiet as we lugged another 96,000 pounds of rice to Phnom Penh but we all winced when black puffs of smoke signaled more hits in the city as we maneuvered for our landing.

John came into the cockpit and as all eyes latched onto him he shook his head. "We're doing everything we can but there's some complications," he said. "If we put out an 'APB' the wrong person may get wind of it and not only would Andy be arrested and probably interned, but every FANK from low Private to Major that had anything to do with airport security would be sent to the thinnest frontline!"

I thought: *Arrest her or whatever, just keep her from being in the wrong place at the wrong time!*

John went on to say that she'd be okay and someone will find her soon.

Lost in our own thoughts, we sat quietly and watched a Bird C-130 approach us on the taxiway. Then the radio announced the arrival of our "falling shoe" with "All bunnies … incoming!" Even though you know it does no good at all, you can't help but crouch a bit. The C-130 was passing in front of us when the rocket hit right under his number one (closest to us) engine!

The scene turned psychedelic! Our ears were assaulted by the explosion, our eyes knocked out of focus by the shock wave, and a sheet of flame was laid down on the ramp when the badly holed engine puked gallons of fuel and oil. Before we had a chance to react, a large puff of white vapor (fire extinguisher) came out of the engine and it stopped turning and burning. The fire truck blasted out the fire on the ramp in front of us with a shot of high-pressure water and after a quick u-turn, followed the C-130 to their offload area. Our ears hadn't stopped ringing yet when the Old Couple came out and began sweeping up shrapnel! The final scene in this mini-nightmare came when the C-130 departed for U Tapao on the remaining three engines.

All buttoned up and ready to go we checked one more time and John shook his head indicating we were still without Andy. Almost reluctantly, we went through the motions and were on our way back to Saigon.

The next run was to be the last of the day and Jim and I thought about riding back up on another airplane to be on hand if Andy showed up. The final vote was unanimous. Handing Big John two more dumb bodies to worry about would not only be unfair but also useless, and if we got stuck there it would put a real kink in the flow of food to a lot of very needy people. We would just have to be patient and go on as usual, leaving the search to a lot of very capable people.

We had to be thankful that, so far, the day's schedule had been glitch free. We hadn't had any mechanical problems and Pol Pot's punks were holding back a bit. They caused some real damage at the airport but didn't slow us down by more than a few minutes. The damaged C-130 even flew a couple more trips with reduced loads, saving their engine change for the night layover in Thailand.

It was a relief to be on our way again and out of the reach of Grant's condemning scowl. I promised myself I'd find something stupid Grant had done and confront him with it. Nah ... I don't think anything he ever did could top this one.

We noted that once again Neak Luong was marked by smoke and a C-130. Our INS (Inertial Navigation System) mileage counted down to 40 out of Phnom Penh and I tuned Tailpipe's frequency. Taking a deep breath, and ignoring the three pairs of eyeballs and ears pointing my way, I called Tailpipe.

"Tailpipe Bravo, this is Tiger 783 ... 40 out ... level 15."

"Tiger 783, Tailpipe ... roger ... we have an extra Bird overhead November Lima (Neak Luong) at 17 (thousand feet) do you have him in sight?"

We looked and spotted it right away.

"Tailpipe, Tiger 783 ... we have the Bird at 17."

"Tiger 783, Tailpipe ... okay ... other traffic is a Bird about to depart and fighters ... they have been advised ... call 20 out." What a letdown. We had all hoped for something different this time but...

"Tiger 783 this is Tailpipe." Big John's voice!

"Tailpipe, Tiger 783." Please!

"Tiger 783 ... Your Bunny has just come in from the cold."

"This is Tiger 783 ... understand ... Thank You Sir!"

I won't go into detail but there was a lot of loud relief flying around the flight deck for the next minute or so. I hoped the shouting wasn't too obvious when I called Tiger operations in Saigon and said: "This is Tiger 783 ... I have a special message for Grant Swartz ... advise him that we have found the part we have been looking for and will have it with us when we return ... Thanks."

Very soon (it seemed like an hour) we were on the ground and taxiing to the ramp. "All bunnies incoming." Someone said: "Shit!" Maybe it was me. A puff of smoke appeared at Sunnybrook Farm and after the expected thump, someone muttered: "Thank God for small favors!" We stopped on John's signal and he turned toward the bunker.

Like a traffic cop, John motioned with his right hand and Andy came out of the doorway. When she reached John he took her hand and we watched them approach until they disappeared under the nose and in just a few seconds they came into the cockpit. Greg, grinning like a monkey, gave Andy's arm a squeeze, slapped John on the back, and headed outside to do his inspections. John, looking relieved, said: "We'll talk tomorrow," and left. Andy just plopped down in the aft jump seat and stared at us.

She looked like hell! At a glance she was still 20-something but her eyes said she was 80. Lord Jim was the first to say something to her. Touching what turned out to be spots of dried blood on her sleeve, he asked her if she was okay.

She said: "I'll have your shirt cleaned. I think that'll come out."

This time Jim got closer and said: "Fuck the shirt, are you all right?"

She just said: "Yes."

Jim went aft and came back with a cup of ice water. When he handed it to her something ... relief or whatever ... caused her hands start shaking so badly the water was gone before it got anywhere near her mouth. Jim got another and this time he held it for her. I think half made it to her mouth and the rest went down the front of her shirt. She started to say something and then began to cry. No sobbing, just a river of tears running down her face.

I think she had joined our club. It would have been a nice touch if someone could have held her just for a minute or so, but things were moving right along and we were all squared away for departure.

As we taxied to the west end Andy regained some composure and stood up to look outside. Pulling up at the end we waved back at the kids as they put on their usual show of cheering us on. Andy tried to smile and wave back but she lost it again and sat down, tears streaming. Greg fastened her seat belt for her and crawled into his seat as I pushed up the power and released the brakes. Andy didn't say one word all the way back to Saigon.

My conscience had a few things to say: "Look what you set up. A 20 something woman (girl), first time outside the North American continent, and you shove her right into the middle of a slaughterhouse. She should have stayed at the airport as she was told but you should have known she would do this. You have changed her life. Now you'd better hope you haven't changed it too much!"

The rest of the flight was without incident except this time we parked in a different spot. Instead of reloading sounds we heard mechanics opening cowls and various hatches and covers. 783 was going to get a routine check-up by "Doctor" Swartz and his crew (the reason behind the odd schedule today). This was my chance to put the name on the airplane so I said I'd meet everyone in the lobby of the hotel around dinnertime.

When I said that, I had hoped for some kind of reaction from Andy. But no luck. I gave her elbow a gentle squeeze as I helped her into Grant's van but she didn't respond to that either. I didn't think I was the most popular person in her life then, and my guilt kept growing.

It turned out I was flattering myself by assuming Andy was thinking about me at all. Her senses had been seriously overloaded on this day and she was still in a near state of shock. Jim later told me after they got into the company van she grabbed his hand and held it tightly all the way to the hotel. So tight he didn't get any feeling back for at least half an hour! He went up to the CBS office, told Peter what had happened and suggested someone keep an eye on her for a while.

Using a belt loader (what is used to put your bags into the belly), I got into position and carefully painted "Phnom Penh Ph-Nancy" on the side of Tiger 783's nose. I parked the loader and returned to the

Tiger 783 sporting my new hand lettering.

airplane with an SM Oil to sip while I examined my handiwork. It looked great. Grant interrupted with an offer of a ride to the hotel so I said, "See you later, Nancy" and took him up on it.

Grant, like many serious mechanics, had his little collection of superstitions. Among them being: It was good to treat a complex machine as if it were a living thing.

"You and Nancy have bonded," he noted. Grant said he could feel good vibes when we (783 and I) were together. I thought maybe Grant was pulling my leg a bit but he looked serious and it was kind of a nice thought.

During the ride, Grant somewhat apologized for biting us during the "Andy" crisis. He explained as a race car and airplane mechanic he had gotten into the habit of expecting the worst and acting accordingly. I told him I was glad he was mistaken this time but had to agree with everything he had said to us at the time. "It won't happen again," I assured him, "Believe me!"

Maria was startled to see me alone. Luckily I caught myself and didn't say I had stayed at the airport to paint a name on the airplane. It would have taken at least an hour to explain why I would do something like that. I just said we had finished early and I had driven in with a friend.

"Jim's already here?" she asked.

I said: "Yes, he's probably taking a nap."

She relaxed then and after telling me I should also take a nap ("It's good for you"), she sold me a newspaper and gave me two more for Jim and Bob. I offered to pay for these but she spared me the cash outlay by insisting she'd get it from them.

Putting off my nap a while I stopped by the newsroom and talked with Peter. One of his people had checked on Andy and she was sleeping quite soundly. I suggested they go gently with the questions until they could assess her state of mind and he agreed, telling me Jim had given him a pretty good description of what she had been up to.

"Do you guys realize how far out your necks were sticking while this was going on?" he asked, and then: "Why'd you do it?"

I answered by telling him I could give a dozen high-sounding reasons, but basically? She just pissed us off.

After he stopped laughing, I went on to explain that for once I had it in my power to shake up a liberal. So I did it.

What bothered me after the fact was my choice of targets. I now felt that, given enough time, Andy would have moved from the left to somewhere near the center. She was definitely sharp, her only problem being a lack of exposure to the real world.

Peter said: "I think you took care of that problem."

I answered: "Yeah, like cracking eggs with a bulldozer!"

Peter went on to say it wasn't really my fault. An hour and a half stay at the bunker would've been risky but reasonable, and she would have picked up a lot from the people there. "I guess," he said, "you could have made prior arrangements to have her restricted to that area but somebody would probably have nixed the whole thing. No, she did it and I'm sure she'll apologize to you first chance she gets."

I retreated to my room, took my nap and did quite well at it.

I was still tired when the phone hummed. But I was also hungry and when I saw it was 6:30 PM I decided to forgive whoever was on the other end. It was Jim passing on Bob's wake-up call. I agreed to meet them in half an hour for some goodies.

Not feeling too inventive we ended up at our little place around the corner. Bob and Jim opted for omelets but I went after the onion soup again. Really good stuff. When I grumble about the French, I am definitely not picking on their cuisine. A very rich but small chocolate pastry and a dark cup of coffee topped me off.

Of course, we had a lengthy discussion about the day's events. Again I was exonerated when I mentioned my feelings of guilt over exposing Andy to the sights and sounds of a dying city. Bob said he was the Captain and he chose to go along with my plot. Jim, knowing more about Andy than Bob and me, said she was 24 years old and if she chose to be the "Evel Knievel" of lady journalists that was her business.

"You worry too much Larry, she'll be fine," Jim finished.

It was a pleasant Sunday evening as we wandered back to the hotel. Just an occasional flicker of lightning to the north competed with the stars and the blinking of scattered aircraft navigation lights in the dark Southeast Asian sky.

Bon soir Hiram.

17 March 1975

Traffic sounds and the morning sunlight woke me. My watch said 8:15 AM, no wakeup-call! I called Jim and after the sound of a dropped handset plus a few growls I got an answer. I wasn't quite sure what language he was speaking but it sounded kind of like: "Yameerwuzzup?" I said: "Rise and shine," and Jim asked me, in English this time, what was going on. I told him I hoped he knew why we hadn't gotten our calls but it was obvious I was way ahead of him on this one. I told him to go back to sleep and I'd call him back if anything important was happening. I could tell he was taking me up on that as his phone rattled and clunked until he finally found the cradle and hung up.

I jumped a bit when my phone hummed just as I hung up. Bob was on the line and said we would be picked up around 10 AM. Tigers woke him at 5 AM to tell him this and he asked them to let Jim and I sleep in, he would alert us later. The agent told him very heavy shelling at Phnom Penh early this morning had disrupted the schedules. I thanked Bob and let him go so he could say funny things to Jim. After much yawning, scratching, and showering, I almost felt human. The little bit of extra sleep really hit the spot. Hiram had gone to wherever he went every day.

I stopped by the CBS office on my way to the hotel restaurant and was informed Andy was still catching up on her rest but was apparently okay. I asked if anyone had really talked with her yet and the answer was no. Peter wasn't in so I just said "Thanks" and continued on to the restaurant while thinking about the stories Andy will have when she's ready to talk about her big adventure.

The three of us finally found each other and had a run of the mill breakfast.

Early in the morning Nancy prepared to take on a full load of rice.

Jim had awakened at 5 AM and tossed and turned all morning. He finally got back to sleep just in time for my call. Now he was having a hard time getting fully up to speed. I hate it when that happens to me so I was careful not to tease him about it. The van would be there for us shortly so we paid up and headed for the lobby.

When Bob and I arrived at the airplane Jim led us to the number one engine and pointed to where a piece of shrapnel had buried itself in the cowling. About the size of a fifty-cent coin it was lodged so tightly that Grant said it would be a major job to remove it. As it wasn't near anything vital he decided to just leave it where it was. Years later, whenever I was around Nancy I would show other pilots this piece of embedded Red Chinese steel and come up with a war story or two.

Everything seemed too quiet today. I've had flights between San Francisco and Los Angeles that were more exciting but as I said earlier, instead of relaxing you just slowly wind up knowing there's something coming your way sooner or later. When and what are the only variables.

As we pulled in to the ramp at Phnom Penh, Big John pointed to where I had painted the name and raised his hand with fingers in the OK position.

John came into the cockpit and asked about Andy. He was relieved to hear she seemed to be okay. "That girl saw things that no one should ever have to see," he said. Then he asked if we had talked to her yet and after we said no, he said she was going to have some real stories to tell.

"Who's Nancy?" John asked next. I explained and he thought it great to not have to say 783 again.

The heavy shelling had been just off the north side of the airport but Tailpipe had closed the entire airport as a precaution. John said it was "something else" as it was all 105 stuff and lots of it (it was still dark and the shooters didn't have to worry about dust). He didn't know what the target was supposed to be unless it was the airport and the spotter was calling the shots in the wrong place. This was probably a prevue of coming attractions when it really rained. Damn!

I used "Tiger 783" when I called Tailpipe and said we were ready to taxi. "Nancy this is Tailpipe ... cleared to 05 without delay ... we have one Bird inbound ... just checked 20 out ... he'll be using 05."

"Tailpipe this is 7 ... correction ... Nancy ... understand ... we're moving."

I guessed the name change was official, at least on this end. We were now the "Tiger called Nancy."

The second trip (last for the day) went well and we wondered if the Rouge were sleeping in after spending the wee morning hours terrorizing a small village called Pochentong and a nearby market. "Pochentong" translated as a place where a Chinese man had planted a tree. It was also the name of the airport. John told us there had been quite a few casualties. They were all civilian.

Back in Saigon, Bob went to Gary's office to retrieve a message operations had told him about. Jim and I continued on to the "trough" for our daily ration and while we were sipping our SM Oil Bob joined us and said he'd been fired! The Director of Flight Operations, Captain Oakley Smith, was back in town and would be our new leader while he tried the shortcut takeoffs at Phnom Penh. Bob seemed really disappointed but he assured us (not very convincingly) that it was only the free cold beer he'd miss. He would ride to the hotel, pack, check out and return to the airport in time for the late afternoon flight to Bangkok.

We'd been through a lot together and Jim and I sad to see him go, but Oakley "Go-Go" Smith was always fun to fly with. Another excellent pilot and all-around good guy (Tigers had a lot of them). The good news Bob told us was another crew had arrived and we would just fly two trips in the morning plus have the next day (Wednesday) off! Great!

Maria met us at the hotel and when Bob told her he was going home she told him how smart he was and he should try to get us to go with him. I told Maria: "We would, but who could leave behind such a beautiful girl?" That got me a dirty look over instant pink cheeks.

The van was going to wait for Bob so we shook hands and wished him a pleasant trip home. I almost got a little choky.

Peter was just inside the door as I looked in on CBS. He asked if I would have time after a nap for a CBS radio interview. I told him how we had enjoyed some extra sleep this AM so I could skip my nappie today. "Okay, we can do it in your room?" I said "Sure" and followed him into the office while he got his notes and recorder.

I about jumped out of my skin when a series of shrieks, shouts, and laughter erupted behind me! Peter's long-lost Vietnamese photographer, Mike (I think), had made it home from Ban Me Thuot! He looked scruffy, dirty, and tired but was obviously happy as hell. It had been a week and one day since anyone had heard from him and there must have been at least six people all trying to hug him at the same time.

Finally ... some good news for a change! I just stood back and smiled while I felt the warmth of this reunion.

Peter got his interview which was mostly about civilians being pounded by the invading factions and why. I hoped I hadn't sounded too dumb or naive. Later, I listened to a copy of that tape and it actually wasn't too bad.

Jim and I went out and found a place that specialized in steaks. I hadn't bitten anything red for a while so I enjoyed a rare T-bone accompanied by a baked potato and a nice salad. Excellent! I think I remember Jim wallowing in a thick slice of prime rib with ... french fries?

We found our way back to the hotel and checked out the CBS office. Sure enough, a debriefing (welcome back Mike party) was underway and we went into the room while looking around for Andy. It's always interesting to be stone-cold sober in a room full of sad-happy imbibers. You're on a different wave length. If we hadn't been scheduled to fly the next morning we'd have been consuming our share so I don't mean to put anybody down but, it was ... "interesting."

Andy was sitting with Udo Nesch! As we approached this odd couple we were startled when Andy loudly said: "Oh no, oh my God!" and started to cry. Knowing these two were sworn enemies, Jim and I moved in their direction ready to defend our fair maiden. When we were close enough to hear everything, we realized they weren't fighting as usual, but were comparing experiences!

They now seemed to be the best of friends and it was obvious Andy was living proof the old adage was true: "A liberal is just a conservative that hasn't been mugged yet!" We knew she had been royally "mugged" by the Khmer Rouge in Phnom Penh!

When it was obvious we were standing over them, Udo looked up and we saw tears running down his cheeks! I was beginning to believe the salt water of oceans originated with tears shed during wars!

I hadn't seen so many grown people cry since my Mother took me to see the movie *Bambi* when it first came out.

Andy spotted Jim and immediately jumped up to squeeze the breath out of him. It didn't take too much imagination to see that Andy's adventure had marked the beginning of a beautiful friendship. One could tell Jim hadn't quite accepted this arrangement yet as he looked a bit embarrassed by her actions, but although his face was red, he was smiling.

Andy never did tell too much about what she had seen and done on her excursion to downtown Phnom Penh. What she saw was already well covered press-wise (though the rest of the world ignored the dispatches) and when asked what she did she started to tell us how she stopped to help a French MD at an aid station (the blood spots on her shirt) but finished by breaking down and crying for several minutes. Everyone soon learned to avoid talking about it unless she brought it up.

Andy did mention she was deeply bothered when she noticed the only military presence in the city were guards at the rice depot and the wounded. She could understand how a civilian bystander might be accidentally run over by the war machine but to specifically target unarmed men? Women and children? No! How could the rest of the world allow Pol Pot, this mad dog Asian "Adolf Hitler," to murder thousands of his own people in cold blood?

She wasn't by any means the only one pondering that question!

A cheer went up as someone remembered what day it was and proposed a toast to Saint Patrick. Of course some wag suggested re-incarnating the "good auld Sod" and bringing him to Southeast Asia to chase away the "snakes" around here.

It was getting to be our bedtime so Jim and I begged forgiveness for leaving such a fine party so early and said our good nights. Andy held our hands to her face and after giving each a kiss proceeded to cry again! She wiped her eyes, smiled a good night, and turned away to rejoin the party.

Jim headed for the elevator and as I walked toward my room I met the second-floor room boy. He smiled and shook his head as the off-key strains of "Danny Boy" reached us.

After I let myself into my room I checked on Hiram. He was not around and I wondered if he was at the party looking for spills.

Lights out, I laid listening to a bad rendition of "Irish Eyes" while thinking how nice it was to hear the word "Smiling." It wasn't too hot that evening and I could have closed the transom above the door but I would have no trouble sleeping with these happy sounds tickling my ears for a change. Luckily, except for us early birds, it was not that late so I doubted anyone would complain.

18 March 1975

Another late start. We'll begin our work day around lunchtime. We could have stayed at the party! Actually I was glad we hadn't as I felt pretty damn good when I woke up. I knew I wouldn't have been able to say that if we'd laughed, cried, and drank till the late hours. We'd have plenty of chances to hurt ourselves later.

Captain Oakley Smith, Jim, and I stopped by Steve's Place on the way to the airport where we had our brunch of burgers and picked up Tailpipe's order of the day. Oakley didn't need all the schooling we had given Bob as he had checked our operation just last week. He *was* a bit apprehensive about the situation at Phnom Penh as he had only been there once before as an observer and that was before things had become so dicey. We told him we hoped his adrenaline pump was in good working order.

At the office we went over extrapolated charts that I felt were meaningless when applied to our "short" takeoff capability. I reminded Oakley that every takeoff we had made at Phnom Penh was short and the unused runway we always put in front of us was just a shooting gallery for the Rouge. He said: "We were just trying to be careful as possible but you're right. Let's just go there and do it!" We wrapped up the rest of the paperwork and went out to say good day to Nancy.

On the way, Oakley said he'd like us to alternate flying complete round-trips instead of each specializing in the legs we flew. He felt there would be enough time for him to take over if necessary. I wondered if I would remember how to land a heavy airplane. Rats! I'm going to lose half the fun approaches and landings at Saigon.

Captain Oakley Smith, senior director of flying, strains against a 5,500-pound pallet.

Everything was ready so after a quick briefing on tire condition from Grant, we climbed aboard, settled in, did the checklists, and soon had four normal starts.

Saigon ground control gave their approval of our intent to taxi to runway 25 Left and Grant gave his usual crisp direction to get us out of our parking area, ending with a salute and a thumb up. I think Oakley was impressed.

Following the (now) usual delay for military traffic we were cleared for takeoff and were very quickly on our way. The takeoff did feel different to me. Nancy came unglued nicely, but of course, not nearly as spirited as when she was empty. I'd had my own little niche and Oakley had to spoil it by insisting I share the fun and do some "work" for a change.

Oakley was working the radios and when he called 40 miles out of Phnom Penh to Tailpipe, things became a little confusing.

"Tailpipe Bravo this is Tiger 783 ... level 15 thousand ... 40 out."

"Nancy this is Tailpipe ... understand ... traffic is TIA departing shortly ... fighters know you're inbound ... call 20 out."

Before I could say anything Oakley said: "Tail–pipe Bravo this is Tiger 783."

During the expected hesitation I quickly said: "It's Nancy, Oakley. We're Nancy." That got me a really strange look from Oakley then he remembered our conversation at the Chinese restaurant about naming the airplane for my wife.

"Tailpipe Bravo this is Nancy."

"This is Tailpipe ... do I have two airplanes at 40 out?"

"Tailpipe ... negative this is Nancy or 783 ... whatever ... we're coming up on 20 out."

"Nancy, Tailpipe ... roger ... cleared to descend your discretion expect runway 23."

"Tailpipe this is Nancy ... understand." I pulled the power back and Oakley continued with: "Leaving 15 thousand."

My face was a little red as I apologized for not telling Oakley about the change in call signs. It was true when I said I had simply forgotten about it. He just smiled and remarked how neat it was to have a name instead of a stupid number. I felt better after he said that and went back to the job of getting "Nancy" safely back to earth. As I lined up on my approach to runway 23, the TIA DC-8 lifted off on their way back to Thailand.

After touchdown I sorely missed light weight and long runways while we ground to a brake-warming stop. Oakley took over and his driving combined with Big John's signals soon had Nancy into position for unloading.

Jim and I had raised Oakley's concerns about "incoming" and he was wearing a properly zipped flak jacket while scanning the horizon for black or brown puffs of smoke. Not a peep from the radio about bunnies. Even the city was enjoying a day where the only rumble came from painfully empty human guts.

The Cambodian boss man came into the cockpit to say hello and we introduced him to Oakley. "Is he a good pilot?" asked our Cambodian friend. Lord Jim answered: "No, but he will be after we teach him how." That produced a toothy laugh and he reached up and patted a smiling Oakley on the shoulder. "I say you should fire these guys, OK? They don't respect old guys enough." With that, he said he'd see us later and returned to the cabin to watch the last pallets of rice leave the airplane. When that happened he gathered up a can of cold pop for each of his men and rode down on the loader.

"Doors closed and checked," came from Greg and checklist complete I started number one and two engines. There was a slight breeze favoring runway 23 and a Bird C-130 was going to be using that runway for landing so we had our conditions in place to try the shortest section of runway for our departure. This meant our actual useable runway would be 3,800 feet long!

This was to be my takeoff, but under the circumstances, Oakley said he'd do the honors this time. Briefing finished, I got Tailpipe's blessing, we pulled onto the runway, made a sharp left turn and stopped, facing the west end. Logic told us this takeoff would be just like all the others we had gone through. We would travel about 3,000 feet on the ground and then gracefully leap into the warm Cambodian air.

Logic aside, we felt a little uneasy when we could clearly see the end of our takeoff area from where we sat. The kids at the west end were even starting to wave as they anticipated our taxiing down to wave back at them. What a thrill they had coming!

All of us were mentally reviewing the charts and figures we had so painstakingly sorted through while planning this experiment and the same figure kept popping up: Three thousand eight hundred and no/100 feet.

Oakley indicated he was satisfied by pushing the throttles up a bit and when the engine instruments indicated all were well and stabilized he released the brakes and called for Jim to set max power. Acceleration was impressive as usual and in just a few seconds we were nicely airborne with room to spare. For once, logic and science had triumphed over luck and superstition!

Oakley was known for having a generous smile but he was literally beaming now. I beamed back as I called Tailpipe. I asked how the takeoff looked. "Like a giant dragster," John replied. "She really got up and went!"

Oakley then said: "It's your airplane" and when I indicated I was in control he went back to being my helper.

This was great, no more time- and nerve-consuming long runs to the end of the runway while feeling like a nude walking down a city street at high noon! Hey Mister Pot, you're going to have to try a lot harder from now on! Up yours.

Leveling at 16,000 feet I raised the landing gear then accelerated toward Saigon and another 48 tons of rice.

Oakley enjoyed watching the descent, approach, and bush-style landing. He also agreed with the idea of avoiding low altitude clouds by a healthy margin but remarked it was not perfectly "legal" under the "instrument flight rules" laid down by the FAA. We filled him in on the regional FAA administrator's approval of our technique and described that gentleman's ride with us to Phnom Penh and back.

Time on the ground was fairly short this time and Oakley soon had us in our lazy left-hand circles to gain altitude out of the Saigon area. Nearing Neak Luong we saw two Bird C-130s, one dropping chutes and the other circling wider and a little higher. We hadn't seen that arrangement before and we were led to assume the drop zone must have shrunk in size to the point where only one aircraft at a time could do business there. It won't be much longer. No smoke.

"Tailpipe this is Nancy … level 15 … 40 out."

"Nancy, Tailpipe … roger … Blue 46 just called 40 out, we have a Bird on final, and fighters have been advised … expect 23 … call 20 out."

"Tailpipe, Nancy … understand."

Oakley hadn't heard of Blue 46 and he wondered if there would be a conflict when we arrived at the same time. I said Blue 46 was a vintage C-46 and Oakley, knowing all about that type of aircraft, figured we would be there for a while before Blue 46 arrived.

"Tailpipe this is Nancy … 20 out."

"Nancy, Tailpipe … roger … descend your discretion … plan on 23."

Oakley pulled the power back.

"Tailpipe, Nancy … out of 15 … runway 23."

"Nancy, Tailpipe … roger … your traffic is a Bird just departing via 23 … not a factor."

"Nancy."

No news for bunnies? It's really quiet today. Oakley is getting more relaxed while Lord Jim and I are thinking about stuffing some TP in our shorts! C'mon Rouge Rats, throw in just a little one so I can breathe normally again.

As I reported approaching the palace Tailpipe cleared us to land. Oakley smoothly rolled out of the wide left turn putting us right in the slot for runway 23. As the TV tower slid by to our right I told him we'd blindfold him next time so he'd have a challenge.

After we were parked and the offload had commenced, Oakley went aft to pee and when he came back he removed his flak jacket before he sat down. "Those things are uncomfortable as hell in this heat," he said. He added that the shelling wasn't nearly as bad as he'd been led to believe.

It was hotter than usual and Big John was hardly setting a good example as he sat on a makeshift seat he had created using his steel helmet and folded up flak jacket. Oakley asked us why we didn't take off the jackets when things were quiet. "You can always put them on if there's a warning." I lamely said we weren't always warned in time to do anything but cringe and Oakley just shrugged and started writing something in a spiral notebook.

I was staring outside at Big John when it happened! For some reason John looked up. He threw his hat like a Frisbee and the rest was a blur. Like some kind of night club act he grabbed his jacket with one hand, pulled on the helmet with the other, and in a blink he was fully armored and trying to make himself as small as possible!

I slid down in my seat, popped the harness and said: "Shit! Down everybody!" Oakley just stared at me as Greg threw a jacket at him. Then Cambodians shouting and … *Blamm!* Shrapnel and shock wave arrived together!

The radio came to life and spouted: "All bunnies … incoming." This reverse warning happened more than once and I didn't like it. You didn't know if someone was late with the call or were trying to warn of another round headed your way!

This time, once again, it turned out to be a late call. I was beginning to believe in miracles as word spread that, also once again, serious injuries or damage failed to happen.

Oakley was now up to speed on the "whys" of flak jackets.

The unloaders re-organized and finished their job, Oakley soon had all four engines running, and I got the takeoff clearance from Tailpipe.

This time we would taxi out and turn to the right where we'd be looking at about 6,000 feet of runway ahead of us for our departure. Damn, this was good! About the only downside to all this was the fact that from now on we would seldom get a chance to check on our West End Kids. Even that wasn't all bad as the Rouge would have one less target in the west end area.

After takeoff, when things quieted down a bit, Oakley asked Jim and I how long we'd been doing this. I guessed he hadn't really thought about it before as he seemed surprised when I said we had been here since day one, March 2nd. Jim checked his log and added: "46 missions." "As soon as I can dig up a couple of replacements you guys are outta here," Oakley said.

I had to answer a request from Saigon Center then. Oakley said we'd talk more while we consumed our daily ration of SM Oil. *Why wasn't I happy about what I just heard? What the hell is wrong with me?!*

To get my mind off the subject I started a good-natured critique of Oakley's performance: "You put the flaps down too soon. Now you're going to have to add some power to get through your turn to final." "You couldn't call it that close," Oakley answered. Lord Jim piped up: "Oh yes he could!" Oakley to me: "Okay smartass, next time you do this and even touch the throttles before we get to 400 feet the first round will be on you." I said, "You're on!"

Oakley did a great job. I was ready to offer an excuse for the thumpy landing (it's hard to get a smooth landing out of an empty [light] airplane) but he slicked it on really nice. I think Nancy liked him.

SM Oil in hand we had our discussion about Jim and I leaving. I had done some thinking since Oakley brought it up and I said I would gladly go home on one condition: I would be allowed to return in two weeks.

Oakley turned to Lord Jim and raised his eyebrows when Jim said: "Me too." Jim and I had never talked about this and I was pleasantly surprised to find he felt the same as me. It would be a shame to break up a team.

Oakley seemed genuinely puzzled so I added (to Jim's nods) that we felt we were helping our friends. We didn't know many of them by name but we had gone through some real crap with them and they were friends! We couldn't just walk away knowing they were still in trouble and still needed us. I was aware someone else could fly an airplane full of rice but we knew the drill. How would we feel if someone was hurt, or worse, because they didn't know some stupid little thing that we did?

I caught myself and said: "End of speech. It's a very hard thing to explain."

There was a moment of silence, then I said as there were enough pilots here that could do the job as well if not better than us, I had to admit that none of the above were reason enough to ignore our families and get shot at on a daily basis.

We had often talked about the day we could get the hell out and go home but when Oakley actually offered that day I almost panicked. I didn't understand what had happened to me (us) but something had screwed with our good sense. After I stumbled through this silly explanation Oakley said he thought he understood, but when our replacements arrived we would go home. After two weeks if we still felt the same way he would personally arrange our return to Saigon.

"Here's to ya," he said as he raised his bottle of SM Oil in our direction.

Looking back, I'm sure Oakley felt certain we'd change our minds once we were with family and familiar surroundings but he would have been wrong. To this day I don't understand what had happened to us. Maybe I'll run into a good shrink some day and be enlightened.

Maria was a little grumpy while she handed out our newspapers but I asked her anyway. "How would you like to have some lunch with us tomorrow and then we'll go shopping, okay?" She said "You kidding? You really got a day off?" I nodded my head and she lit up. With a big smile she looked at Oakley and said: "You guys gotta good boss now!" Not wanting to lower her appraisal of Oakley I didn't bother explaining he had little to do with this great news. She said she'd start looking for us around 10 but, her smile turned to a gentle frown, we were to sleep for as long as we could. [Yes, Mother!]

Oakley had a message from one of our Ops people that said the three of us were invited to drinks and dinner at a private club somewhere in Saigon. Something different like this sounded downright exciting! We would meet in the hotel lobby after a short nap and the mandatory "after-sweat" shower.

My heavy burden of good news was lightened a bit when I stopped by the CBS office. There I received word that NVA forces had overrun the city of Quang Tri (just south of the border between North and South Vietnam) and were about to break through a line held by the South Vietnamese at the My Chanh River. This was about 25 miles from the city of Hue and refugees from that area were pouring down Highway 1 into Danang. Peter was very worried about his in-laws now. I quietly left for my room.

It felt good to lay down but a nap didn't happen. It was like the night before Christmas only the visions dancing in my head were the exact opposite of "sugar plums," whatever that would be.

Freshly showered and clothed I made my way to the lobby. In just a few minutes at least six of us gathered and we rounded up as many cabs. I was at the mercy of my driver as we wound this way and that through the darkening streets of Saigon.

In just a few turns I was totally lost but we soon pulled up in front of a row of what would be called "brownstones" in New York City. Even though the little blue cabs had scattered when leaving the Caravelle they all parked in a row within seconds of each other! Amazed at this show of coordination, everyone gathered on the sidewalk chatting about pilot things and the latest war news. Our man from Tigers led us into what looked from the outside like someone's city residence but inside we found a plush dining area overlooked by a bar in a loft to the rear. This was definitely not our Mom and Pop place!

We reluctantly (Maria would say: "Yeah sure") went up the stairs like migrating salmon and moved to the bar. As the only crew not flying tomorrow, Oakley, Lord Jim, and I sipped Johnny Walker Black and felt really guilty ("Yeah sure") while the others nursed their Virgin Mary, pop, or whatever.

After coming up with solutions for all the problems of mankind we were told our table was ready so we went back downstairs to the dining area.

The food and service were fantastic. We were tended by a team of really lovely waitresses and a chef that came out to be sure we were all happy with his handiwork. Yes!

For a short while I was able to push the gritty side of our present life to the far back of my mind. That was much appreciated. Thanks everyone, wherever you are.

The three of us and the Tiger agent lingered for a while at the bar after saying good night to the pilots of tomorrow. The good food and spirits soon got to Jim and me so we also said thanks and good night. Someone was on the ball as two cabs were waiting for us when we went out the door. That's class!

Once again the cabs went by different routes but arrived at the Caravelle within seconds of each other. After we agreed that the first up (within reason) would wake the other, Jim headed for the elevator while I crawled up the stairs.

The damn sleepies had hit me hard so I slipped past the CBS office grateful that no one spotted me. I didn't feel like talking to anyone.

When my head dented the pillow I heard three "bumps" of artillery then slipped into a dream-free sleep.

19 March 1975

South Vietnam: Over one million refugees have now arrived in and around Danang from the north. Most have hopes of getting aboard a boat or barge that will take them to Saigon but there is a severe shortage of larger vessels. Adding to the panic, Highway 1 between Hue and Danang is now being shelled by NVA artillery units to the west. Survivors will later tell of entire families lying dead, victims of the artillery or the stampede of humanity trying to run from the shelling. Passersby would neatly arrange the remains beside the road with their belongings and cover them with blankets or straw mats.

Dammit! Wide awake at 5 AM. I knew we should have stayed out and played for a while last night.

Maybe that wasn't the problem; there was a lot of shooting going on southwest of Saigon. Where wasn't there shooting going on in South Vietnam or Cambodia? Grateful the gun I was listening to was on my side, I slowly relaxed as I kept track of the numbers. After ten sets of three flashes and "bumps" I went back to sleep.

I slowly woke up to muffled traffic sounds and semidarkness. I thought it was awfully hot for early morning then I realized I had pulled a pillow over my head. It was 10 AM and a bright sunny day. While I was brushing cobwebs off my brain the phone hummed. When I answered Jim said, "10 o'clock, resurrection time." He had tried calling me earlier and when I didn't answer he thought I had left already.

After he spotted Maria outside at ten he tried again.

Awake and hungry, I zipped through the morning clean-up ritual and headed downstairs. Jim and Maria were outside chatting when I showed up. Jim said he and I had picked where to eat last time so Maria insisted on her choice today. She would not settle for anything less than a hamburger with all the trimmings! She had never heard of Steve's and although suspicious Jim might be tricking her into something vegetarian, she agreed to go along with his suggestion that we try it. I didn't object as this meant she could have her burger and I could order a good old-fashioned breakfast. Jim was also in need of something hearty. He had coffee with Oakley earlier but nothing to eat. Oakley accepted a rain check from Jim on the shopping spree and went to the Tiger office at the airport.

We tried to order up two cabs but "Miss Miser of Saigon" wouldn't hear of it. What caused the problem was Jim starting the argument by saying we'd done it before and … that was enough. Maria said if we'd done it before we could do it again! She would ride in front with the driver.

A burger by Steve, a large order of fries, and half a bottle of ketchup later, Maria was so mellow she even agreed to drink the glass of milk we'd ordered for her.

On the ride back to the hotel and the shopping area along Tu Do Street, I said I was impressed by the way Renault engineers had designed a car that didn't need seatbelts. Jim asked what I meant and I said, "We could hit a brick wall at 60 miles an hour and our bodies wouldn't move half an inch!" He answered, "Stop talking so much, you're making my ears pop."

Obviously Maria hadn't the foggiest notion of what we were laughing about but she and the driver smiled as they chatted in their own language.

Maria was really embarrassed when Jim and I caught everyone's eye by pretending we couldn't stand up after we got out of the taxi. "Don' do that! Everybody's looking at you!"

A little old lady stopped very close to Lord Jim and bent over a bit as if to see his face. Maria about had a heart attack when Jim straightened up and gave the lady a hug. When the woman just smiled and returned the squeeze, Maria relaxed and her frown changed to a smile. They exchanged a few words, then the lady nodded to us and continued on her way. "She say you guys are good looking," Maria explained. Jim looked at me and said: "That poor old girl needs glasses."

A short, civilized day at work followed by a good night's sleep and we were almost fun to have around. Phnom Penh seemed far, far away.

Maria steered us down Tu Do Street a couple of blocks to a fair-sized store that had all kinds of stuff to poke through. Along with the popular Vietnamese porcelain elephants of various sizes, they had carved wooden boxes, wall hangings, vases, and enough miscellaneous bric-a-brac to keep any hard-core garage saler in ecstasy for at least an hour or two.

My wife liked candlesticks so I zeroed in on the display of brassware. We had been told the brass here was of the highest quality as it was cast of melted down empty shell casings from the USA. Not quite swords into plowshares but a step in the right direction.

I picked out a pair that looked good and while I was examining them Maria came over and said: "You like those?" I said I thought they would do nicely and Maria checked the price—10,000 (piasters). "You gonna pay in green?" she asked, meaning U.S. dollars. I hadn't bothered to change any money so I said yes. While she ran the calculator that I'm sure was implanted in her head, I came up with, at the official rate of 500p to the dollar: 20 US dollars. Maria nodded toward the gentleman running the place and said, "Give him ten dollars." I'm not good at haggling anyway but this seemed really out of line. "That's half-price, he won't take that!" Now I got a lesson in higher math (larceny?).

"He's mark the price in p's, right?" I nodded. "He's not gonna take your ten to the bank. He's gonna take it to a street changer (black market) and get 8,000p for it." I nodded again, beginning to see the light. "He's ask 10,000p and you give him 8,000p, that's a good deal!" Then she said, " You sure you like these things?" I said my wife will, and Maria changed the subject by asking, "Is you wife pretty?" I answered by saying she must be, she's got me. "Yeah, sure. You gonna buy some more stuff?" I said I'd just get the candlesticks for now and come back just before we left for home (I didn't).

She asked Jim if he was getting anything and he said he would also wait till later so Maria told the manager-clerk we had what we wanted. When I offered the ten dollar bill he pushed it away and said, "No, no, twenty!" Maria glared at him and in a staccato burst of Vietnamese explained the deal. He growled something under his breath, took my candlesticks, wrapped them in newspaper, and after carefully scrutinizing my tenner, handed them to me.

On the way out of the store Maria nodded and said something pleasant to the man but he just growled again and waved her away as he turned his back.

Some old hands have told me since that this was a common thing in Southeast Asia. The man was probably Maria's uncle or something and they had this routine they would go through to sell goods to tourists. I don't think so. I think Maria knew I would probably cough up 20 bucks for candlesticks that would have been a bargain at 30 dollars! I've never heard of a merchant anywhere who would take a large cut like that just for a quick sale.

The candlesticks are on our mantel right now. Thanks Maria, my wife really likes them.

We continued down Tu Do almost to the Saigon River before wandering back in the direction of the hotel. Neither of us bought anything else but we now knew where to go for various kinds of goodies.

Maria didn't seem to mind just window shopping but when Jim and I seemed interested in farm equipment she wondered aloud: "How you gonna get a tractor home from here?" What had caught our attention was a showroom stocked with bright red machinery bearing a well-known USA trademark. It wasn't the heavy-duty stuff you'd see in North America, but it was obvious someone was ready to get with some serious farming. There were several modestly dressed Vietnamese men inside kicking tires and seriously discussing the merits of different pieces.

We were impressed with the high hopes these people displayed, and were depressed that we knew it was all going to end soon.

When we arrived back at the Caravelle, Maria said she had to go pick up her newspapers. Jim and I heartily thanked her and she thanked us for the "goood" hamburger. She and a couple of her cronies took off up the street and we went inside.

Peter had left a note in my message box asking if he could do an interview for CBS TV. We went up to the office and Peter called us right in. Would we do it? "Sure, when?"

"What are you doing right now?" He asked. When we answered "Not a thing," he said to meet him and a cameraman at the entrance of the upstairs lounge that was also the last stop of the elevator. Jim and I split for our rooms to neaten up a bit and check for spinach on a tooth, that sort of thing. I had a zillion thoughts I wanted to share with my fellow Americans but not one came out of hiding during the elevator ride.

Jim was already there when I got out of the elevator. Peter brandished a large key ring and after finding the right key, opened a door that guarded the stairway leading to the roof of the hotel. I'm not sure but I think the Caravelle was ten stories high and it stood above all but the Continental Palace Hotel across the street. What a view!

Peter quickly went over the main questions he was going to ask and assured us he had screened his notes making sure there was nothing classified in them. He did warn us to not volunteer anything that shouldn't be said. The tape would be edited but it would make it easier for him if we simply answered his prompts and queries.

I would look back on this later and realize how fortunate it was it came up so suddenly. We didn't have a chance to really think about the possibility that millions of people might see and hear us! I can imagine it now. "Yup, my name is um … (notes!) … Larry?" Maybe not that bad but we found the big lens of that camera intimidating enough without the other thoughts. Like the radio interview this didn't turn out too bad.

It was amusing that somewhere between Saigon and New York City our names were switched in the subtitles. Jim's not a bad name, I've certainly been called worse, but I wasn't sure if I wanted to be from New Jersey.

We wandered back down to Peter's office and as we entered Peter was introduced to a visitor. Peter in turn introduced Jim and me to Roar Bjerknes, a young journalist with The Sonnmorsposten news service in Alesund, Norway. He turned out to be a very pleasant chap and we hit it off right away. Of course, we compared notes on the beautiful scenery of our home areas (mine being Washington State). Roar very quickly came up with a gift for me, a wonderfully illustrated hardcover book about his home town of Alesund. I vowed that I would visit him as soon as I could. I never did.

After an early dinner Jim and I checked out the debriefing room. The usual suspects were there and Andy showed obvious pleasure when she saw Lord Jim enter the room. She steered him off to the side and held both his hands as she chatted gaily away about something. Blushing just a little now, Jim looked in my direction and shrugged. Andy followed his line of sight and gave me a big smile and wave.

On my own, I talked to Udo for a few minutes, then Roar joined us. Udo started to introduce us but I said we'd already met. Udo pointed out that Roar's main interest was Phnom Penh and mentioned I had taken one reporter up there already. "Maybe he will do the same for you, Roar." Udo spotted someone else he wanted to talk to and left us to discuss Phnom Penh. Just thinking about our "exciting" experience with Andy gave me a sudden desire for the stiff drink our schedule wouldn't allow us (we had an early-morning go tomorrow).

Roar looked so hopeful I felt I at least should explain why we couldn't do that again. As I told the story he looked properly concerned about Andy and when I got to the part about her possible arrest and internment he was amazed she would go in the face of a situation as serious as that. There I had to back up a bit and admit I (we) hadn't thought about the possibility and Andy had since convinced us she would not have risked it had she known.

I thought for a moment about what I had just said and did an about-face. "Be in the lobby a little before 6 AM and we'll ask Captain Smith about your going with us, okay?" Roar cracked a big smile and shook my hand, "Thank you Lars" (I had told him about my wife's nickname for me). Then he reassured me by telling me his newspaper knew he might be in harm's way sooner or later on this trip and he was not doing this against their wishes. All his paperwork was up to date and he would be ready to return on our next flight out, no downtown! I warned him there might be one last hitch: Big John would have to approve. If he didn't, Roar would have to stay on the airplane and return directly to Saigon.

Roar's enthusiasm wasn't dampened a bit as he said just the flight alone would be more than he had hoped for.

I realized Andy and Jim had quietly moved in when Andy spoke. "Don't go into the city, Roar. It's a place of death. It's…" She turned away. Roar said he had seen very graphic photos and read unpublished reports out of Phnom Penh and added, "She's going to be messed up for a while."

It was time for Lord Jim and I to take our main nappy so after recommending Roar buy a newspaper from Maria and why, we took our leave.

I paused on my way to bed and sat near the window listening to the evening pre-curfew traffic noises mixed with an occasional rumble of thunder from a spectacular thunderstorm several miles to the west.

Good night God.

20 March 1975

South Vietnam: NVA units have eased somewhat on their frontal assault and are now concentrating on cutting off and trapping South Vietnamese Army and Marine troops in Hue. NVA shelling of Highway 1, between Hue and Danang still choked with civilian refugees, is intensified.

Roar was waiting in the lobby all bright-eyed and happy to be going somewhere. I felt like stomping on his foot or something to put him in a mood that we could live with. While he was showing Oakley an impressive batch of credentials I remembered I hadn't warned him that Oakley didn't know about Andy's little adventure! I stood close by and was ready to launch into a fit of coughing if it became necessary. Later, when we were able to talk, Roar told me that everyone concerned appreciated the risks we took and knew this was not a story to be spread around.

Oakley turned to Jim and I and asked if we had any objections to bringing Roar along. I said it was fine with me, and while trying to keep a straight face, Jim nodded and mumbled: "Me too." Oakley didn't notice our touch of nerves and declared it was time for breakfast. Roar wanted to take some pictures at Steve's but I mentioned there might be someone there on his way to a sensitive job (CIA) that would object. Probably not true, but I think Roar liked the touch of intrigue.

On our way to the airport Roar told us of his travels so far. I don't remember every detail but I think he started this assignment in Bangkok and worked his way through Laos and part of Cambodia before arriving in Saigon. He really wanted to spend some time in Phnom Penh but he was a little late for that. Most of his fellow journalists who had

145

been in that city were now out or leaving shortly. He explained that Pol Pot had imposed a death sentence on anyone who was not Khmer (Cambodian) and Rouge (Communist), this included the press.

Without thinking, I said, "I wish you'd been here to tell that to Andy." He shot a glance at Oakley then said, "It wouldn't have mattered, from what I hear she would have ignored anything said by someone obviously brainwashed by the CIA." To our relief, Oakley was busy looking outside and hadn't been listening.

It seems rude to hide something from a friend but Oakley was in management at the time, and I like to think he would have appreciated our not telling him about it. I know he would have covered for us but it wouldn't have been a nice spot to put him in.

Roar very attentively took in all the details of our "job" while staying out of our way. All in all a very intelligent, curious, thorough, and yet courteous person. Qualities lacking in too many of today's press corps.

Flak jackets were passed out and adjusted. Before Jim came into the cockpit I showed Roar his seat behind Oakley and explained Lord Jim would give a briefing on what to expect. Roar said, "Lord Jim?" Jim came in as I explained the "Lord" part to Roar and he embarrassed Jim a bit by exclaiming that was one of his favorite stories about Cambodia.

Everything went smoothly as usual and we were soon lined up on runway 25 waiting for Saigon tower to give us permission to go get shot at. Roar pointed his camera and snapped a VNAF Chinook helicopter as it passed in front of us.

"Tiger 783, Saigon ... cleared for immediate takeoff."

"Saigon, Tiger 783 ... rolling."

Neak Luong was quiet with no smoke or C–130s in the air above it. The burned-out freighter in the river was the only sign of the malignancy eating the city and its people. For a change, our guest knew way more about Neak Luong than we did. It was fascinating but not encouraging to listen while Roar confirmed all we had heard about the place and then some. I was beginning to wonder about the C–130s when Roar spotted one ahead and to our left heading for the drop zone.

This time Oakley was up to speed on our new call sign.

"Tailpipe, this is Nancy ... 20 out ... 15,000."

"Nancy, Tailpipe ... roger ... descend your discretion ... expect runway 23 ... traffic is one Bird landing shortly ... fighters have been notified ... the stove is warming up and this may be a bad place for bunnies any time now."

Jim said "Shit!" and Oakley looked at me with raised eyebrows. I simply nodded, and he went back to the radio.

"Tailpipe, Nancy ... understand ... Thanks."

I closed the throttles to begin our descent and started to speak. Then, with my mouth half open I saw the reason for the thinly coded message from Tailpipe. Visibility had dropped slightly and I could feel the hairs on my neck stand up as thin rivulets of rainwater began chasing each other up the windshield! My home is in western Washington State so I'm normally not too emotional when it comes to rain. This time I was almost physically ill when I became aware that it was finally here. Our odds worsened with each drop.

Roar was truly amazing! In spite of the fact English was his second language he immediately understood Jim's quick explanation of why 105mm artillery + rain-dust = bad news for everyone in the Phnom Penh area, especially the airport. Jim also told Roar that he'd better plan on returning to Saigon with us on this flight. Roar agreed, but I'm sure he felt disappointment over missing his hour and a half on the ground.

Our anxieties were eased a bit when the rain failed to get serious but you could see it might pick up at any moment. When we had stopped at the ramp Oakley told Roar to go on out with Greg but be ready at any time to either run to the bunker or scramble back into the airplane. Grabbing his camera, Roar eagerly chased Greg to the loader.

Just a couple of minutes later, about 150 yards from us in the direction of Sunnybrook Farm, a huge cloud of dust and brown smoke erupted. That was immediately followed by a sharp "Krack" and the shock wave! All the crud and shrapnel went away from us at a slight angle so no harm was done but there were probably more than a few silent prayers in at least three different languages asking for the shooter's luck (skill?) to remain bad. After about 30 seconds of silence we realized there would not be an "all bunnies ... incoming" announcement!

The offload was about finished and Greg had reboarded when Big John motioned to get our attention. He pointed at his nose and held up five fingers one by one...? Jim turned out to be the charades player of the crew by figuring out John wanted a nose count. Oakley shook his head and held up four fingers and Jim and I started to sweat a little harder. Where was Roar?

John motioned to a FANK officer and after a quick exchange of shouts a ground search was under way. Oakley didn't seem too concerned but Greg, Jim, and I were about to have kittens! Big John didn't look too happy either. Just in case, Greg rechecked the cabin but all he had to say when he returned was the last pallet of rice was about to be offloaded. Genuine panic was about to grab us (the three conspirators) when we saw the Lieutenant appear from behind the bunker with Roar following closely behind. Roar half-saluted the officer with a wave and a smile and trotted out to board the airplane. Oakley did look a little puzzled as he heard three sets of lungs empty at the same time. "You guys worry too much," he said. Followed by: "How could anybody get lost around here? Where could he possibly go?" After a nervous giggle or two Jim and I wholeheartedly agreed that we were being a bit silly.

With Roar safely aboard, the doors closed and checked, and all engines running we taxied to the runway as the light drizzle turned to light rain. Not good! As Oakley turned Nancy to the right to line up for takeoff, I saw another large brown puff rise from just beyond the Tailpipe bunker. A second or two later we all heard a "Thump" but no warning for the bunnies. I remarked about that and Roar said he knew why and would tell us when he could.

Checklists complete, I pushed up the power and when all was stable called for Jim to set max power. I still felt a rush as Nancy quickly accelerated to liftoff speed and I rolled her sharply into a steep climbing right turn. All the bad parts aside, this adventure of ours included some of the most fun flying I had ever experienced! It was hard to believe I was having this fun in one of the largest transport airplanes in the world. What a shame my enjoyment had to be dampened by the circumstances. Oh well, back to work.

Roar was finally able to tell us about the lack of "bunny" warnings. The standing procedure at Tailpipe was to call warnings with rockets but not when 105mm artillery was more than a random shot now and then. The 105 could be aimed accurately if a spotter was available and if no spotter, some accuracy was still possible if the radio announced the arrival of each shell! No one had ever explained that to us but it made sense. I remembered, unlike the rockets, you couldn't see a 105 coming anyway. When it hit, it gave its own warning if you were still alive to hear it.

The rest of this run back to Saigon was routine except for the occasional spit from a radio receiver when lightning discharged its duties somewhere nearby. Our radar showed thunderstorms buried in the murk just to the north of us but the air was smooth. I was able to show off a little during the approach and landing and Roar seemed genuinely interested. He was going to wait with us to see if the situation would improve, allowing him to go back to Phnom Penh.

On the ramp at Saigon we sat in the airplane drinking coffee and talking. The onload had been completed and a quiet hour had passed when the radio came to life.

"Nancy this is Tiger operations" (everyone called us Nancy now except Saigon).

"Tiger Ops, Nancy"

"Nancy, Tiger Ops ... the 105s are still active at PP and Tailpipe has suspended all operations until at least tomorrow morning ... go ahead and close out the book. Grant will be out shortly and will give you a ride to the office."

"Nancy ... will do ... any SM Oil around?"

"Roger ... a few from yesterday."

I clicked the microphone twice to acknowledge and joined Oakley and Jim by stowing my stuff for the day. No, we weren't happy about the break. Tummies desperate for calories were going to grumble their displeasure even louder in Phnom Penh tonight. Many would stop grumbling forever.

We were a somber bunch on the way to the hotel. Even Roar lost his lively enthusiasm that we had thought was a permanent condition. How can a so-called civilized world so deliberately ignore a situation like this?

Oakley was going to have a quick lunch and head back to the airport. Roar had a nap as first priority, then he was going to put his experiences with us in writing to send to his syndicate in Norway. This left Jim and me pretty much on our own so we decided to wander up street to the American embassy for lunch.

We apparently had proper ID as we were readily admitted. After following directions through flat white-walled corridors and a short elevator ride we arrived at the snack bar on the second floor. It was a fresh-air arrangement overlooking a small enclosed area that held a modest-sized swimming pool. We ordered a pair of club sandwiches and a draft beer apiece. The beer came right away and we sipped while quietly looking around.

The swimming pool was occupied by a dozen or so children ranging from about five to fourteen years old. Most of them on the chubby side and all of them bored.

The boys were going through the motions of boys swimming, the occasional cannonball or whatever but without laughter or much noise of any kind. The girls were sitting or standing around trying to look 20ish while those we assumed were the mothers lounged around in the background trying to do the same. Neither were doing well at it.

We found this scene very depressing. In all fairness, I have to point out that this picture may have been a result of the swelling war. Maybe these people were more depressed than we were and were trying their best to act normal.

We brightened somewhat when our sandwiches arrived but that also was a disappointment. Canned ham and chicken with soggy lettuce, generic cheese, and a smear of ballpark mustard all on lightly toasted white bread. The potato chips looked good but on first bite it was obvious they had long ago lost the battle with their mortal enemy, humidity.

Later, I would remark to Jim that if I was an employee of the embassy I would never eat there and I would send my kids to play with Maria and her bunch.

We took our time walking back to the Caravelle along a wide quiet tree-lined street. There was a young boy, about five or six years old, selling a bottle of liquid that looked like weak whiskey. Curious, we stopped and asked him what it was. "Gas," he replied. Puzzled, I took the bottle and sniffed the top. He meant what he said, it was gasoline! The little imp had probably siphoned it out of some MP's jeep while the guy ate his lunch. "You wanna buy?" I handed it back to him and we continued on.

At the hotel we checked for messages, then split for our rooms and naps. I sat at my open window and contemplated the gray day while sipping my warm SM Oil. It hadn't rained here at all and the street was busy as ever. I retreated to the bed where I laid back and thought about many things while listening to the whine of motorbikes and the occasional mating call (toot) of the lesser blue Renault. This all faded as my eyelids gave up and closed.

It wasn't totally dark when I woke from a really good nap so I knew I still had time for dinner or breakfast. When I found my watch on the floor beside the bed I was able to tell it was evening not morning. Dinner it is! I called Jim's room but after many rings (his phone wasn't fixed like mine) I gave up and decided I was on my own tonight. While I showered I was hit with a craving for crunchy tender spring rolls and ice-cold beer.

Chinese restaurants typically cater to families or other groups and our favorite one here in Saigon was no exception. I felt a bit out of place as the waiter led me to their smallest table, set for six, and pulled out a chair for me. He recognized me from before and smiled while handing me a menu. "Cold Tiger beer, right?" I answered "Yes sir," and not bothering to open the menu followed up with, "and a double order of your best spring rolls." He tapped the menu and said, " You missin' a lot of good stuff in here, you sure you just want spring rolls?" I said I'd been thinking about them for a while and only they would do and added: "Next time."

He smiled again and said, "You got it boss, comin' right up!" The spring rolls here would have been called "Lumpia" in the Philippines. About the size of a typical cigar they consisted of a chopped pork-shrimp-vegetable mixture rolled up in several layers of a paper-thin wrapper. All deep fried and served with a rich sweet and sour sauce for dipping. Great stuff!

A pot of tea and some crisp little almond cookies topped me off. After sending my compliments to the chef I made my way down to the street and slowly window shopped my way back to the hotel. My message box yielded a newspaper from Maria and a note saying the wake-up call would be on schedule tomorrow.

I made my way up the stairway and checked for a debriefing but only found Udo and a stranger sharing a quiet conversation over a pair of drinks.

Udo offered me a drink but I asked for a rain check explaining I had to go flying early tomorrow. I said I wished I was a journalist so I could be rich, famous, and not have to work for a living. Udo feigned personal injury then mentioned Jim and Andy were there earlier along with Peter and some others but everyone pooped out early. I was feeling droopy after my meal so I said good night and went to my room.

Even Hiram had come in early and was sitting on the edge of the tub to greet me. I looked out the window for a while but nothing was happening other than a few faraway flickers of lightning.

Say good night Hiram.

21 March 1975

Around 4 AM what sounded like a jeep going as fast as a military jeep could go went past the hotel (and my open window) heading southeast down Tu Do Street.

That brought me to the edge of waking up. A few "bumps" of artillery and the now familiar sound of the AC-119 overhead opened my eyes. Normally, I would be a little grumpy about all this but my long nap yesterday afternoon plus a sound sleep till now had me more rested than I had been since we got here.

I didn't want to feel the crunch of Hiram expiring under my bare foot so I did a kind of shuffle through the dark to the bathroom. Back in bed, I laid back and ran a lot of things through my mind.

I thought about Maria. I was discovering that 13 year old girls seem to be composed of a secret blend of child and woman. Lord Jim and I were her close "adult" friends, and as I pointed out earlier, she also greatly enjoyed "mothering" us and passing out sage advice whenever the opportunity presented itself. In our case, that was often "You go out drinkin?" "A little." "Yeah, sure" or "You keep goin' to Phnom Penh somebody's gonna make a hole in you!"

One of the new pilots was very family oriented with daughters of his own. He also shared Maria's religion (Catholic). The child side of Maria was drawn quickly to this gentle man and he became what she badly needed. A Father. Temporary, but she took whatever she could, when she could. It was strange to hear about our young "woman" pouting like a 10 year old when "Dad" made her finish her soup before she could have dessert. I wondered when she was ever 13. When she was sleeping?

When the time comes, how the hell are we going to extract ourselves from this "Family" we are gathering around us?

Flash ... flash ... flash. Wait a moment, then. Bump ... bump ... bump!

I wonder how I'll feel if whoever replaces me is badly injured ... or worse.

The wake-up call was the usual except for news that Oakley had been replaced by Captain G. "Dick" Riemer, our fourth Captain so far. Maybe Jim and I had better try a different deodorant or something.

Yesterday afternoon Oakley had received word that Dick was on his way here to relieve him. He quickly packed and was at the airport to greet Dick as he stepped off the flight from Manila. After giving Dick an abbreviated briefing at the airport, Oakley was on his way home by way of Bangkok and Tokyo. Oakley left a note at the office for Jim and me saying he had tried to call and say so long but neither of us were in at the time.

He wrote on to say our replacements were on the way, we were doing a fine job, and he would see us sometime soon after we came out. I know Oakley would have flown the ricelift to the bitter end, but as Tiger's Director of Flight Operations he had a busy schedule. With the short takeoff procedure proved and in place he was only here until his replacement arrived.

Dick and I had flown many pleasant trips together and I was looking forward to his joining us on this operation.

Hiram must have been feeling insecure as he stayed much closer as I went through the morning toilet routine. How did he know I was not a threat to his humble existence? I came up with the idea that cockroaches must be like houseflies. They somehow sensed your attitude and would buzz around annoyingly until you reached for the swatter then ... poof! Nowhere in sight. I suppose a scientist would have a good chuckle over such nonsense but it happens. Some would find our relationship a little weird but remember the alternative? Dozens of the critters all over the place! I should point out that the Caravelle Hotel was a clean establishment but certain things are inevitable in tropical areas.

I met Dick in the lobby and when I asked why in the world he volunteered he said he was just curious and didn't want to miss out on any fun. "Oh you're gonna have fun all right," I said. I added: "I just hope your first day is a little gentler than Bob Bax's." We turned to greet Jim as he came out of the elevator, then the three of us went to the van and on to Steve's.

Once again we were relating the same old story to new ears. Dick wondered what kept us here if it was so bad. Good question. Jim and I knew the answer but we had given up trying to put it into words. We just said he would understand after a few trips. I said: "Hey relax, you're with a charmed crew. Twenty hard days, 47 missions and they haven't even scratched us!" Jim reminded me that just the other day Greg had been nipped in the arm by a piece of shrapnel. I countered: "He was with the other crew, and besides it was just a nick. Greg was mainly upset about his good shirt being ruined! He didn't bleed much." Dick looked at me for a moment then said: "Thanks Larry, that's very reassuring."

After we walked the mandatory paper trail we were driven to Nancy. Yes, this time I was careful to relate the "Nancy" story to Dick. Grant met us at the airplane and gave his briefing on tires, etc. Grinning, he said to me: "You guys really wear out Captains. I think you're number five, Dick." I corrected that to four and added it was from them trying to keep up with Jim and me and our rich night life. Grant recalled something I said during a conversation the other day and said: "Drinking warm beer and watching thunderstorms is kinda strenuous. Don't try to keep up with them Dick, just pace yourself."

Dick had me do the flying this time while he watched and learned the profiles. We told the story of Neak Luong and pointed it out when we approached the area. No smoke again but we spotted a Bird C-130 preparing to drop a load into the city. I called Tailpipe at 40 miles out and Dick readied himself to do the 20-mile call. Runway 23 was in use which was good because I could show Dick the most complicated approach with its track near the "forbidden" Palace and the TV tower.

We went through the steep circling descent, tracked around the Palace, and went by the tall antenna tower without hearing a single "bunny" call or seeing any hits in the city. It wasn't raining either. This could turn out to be a rather nice day.

I don't know what it was but something had dulled my edge. Complacency? A good night's sleep, a quiet day, and maybe a little too casual an attitude while impressing Dick with my tour guide skills? Whatever, on short final approach I found myself a little low and a little slow. *No problem! Just add a shot of power. That's right! See? No problem. Too soon! You pulled it back too soon! You idiot!*

Bad landing! Hard landing! Have you ever seen films of navy jets landing on an aircraft carrier? Poor Nancy.

Thank God we didn't blow any tires. The final damage assessment listed my ego as the only casualty but I would've bet hard money that landing showed up on earthquake detection equipment all over the world. I think Dick realized I was mentally lashing myself with barbed wire as he didn't say more than a couple of words. Even Jim was mercifully quiet but I did notice a bit of a smirk when I glanced in his direction.

By the time we arrived at the Tailpipe ramp I was rewarming to the task of describing the sights and pointing out particulars to our new leader. John came up and said a rocket had hit a while ago right where we were sitting now! Otherwise, he said, it had been really quiet so far. Nothing like yesterday. I was relieved when Greg came in and said the brakes were a little hot as usual but everything else was just fine.

The Cambodian boss came in next and noticed we had a new captain. "Where's the gray-haired guy?" he asked. Lord Jim said he and I had fired him: "Just like you said." "No, no, I said he should fire you guys!" the boss answered. He turned, smiling and said to Dick that he's got to get rid of us, "These guys don't respect old guys at all."

The Old Couple were standing a short distance away apparently waiting for us to leave so they could get back to work on the scar the last rocket had left on their ramp. I pointed them out to Dick and they smiled when they saw us looking their way. We had told him their story earlier and now he was seeing them. I had a feeling he was being drawn into our little club already and would not ask again why Lord Jim and I were still here.

The run back to Saigon went smoothly and this time I was paying attention. The descent, approach, and landing were without flaw and Dick started to regain some confidence in his co-pilot. Nancy was so happy with the landing she was purring.

Tailpipe's lunch came aboard, clearance was received, starts were completed, and then it was Dick's turn to drive.

The overcast was thickening and our thoughts were once again about rain and the consequences. We had hopes that the rumor about the Rouge running low on 105mm ammunition was true. If true, it would mean rain would not make such a difference after all.

Going into Phnom Penh, Dick followed the profile perfectly and finished it off with a smooth touchdown. I said: "Oh, I see. So that's how it's done!" Dick was never generous with his smiles but I got one for that. At the ramp, Big John came aboard. Glancing at the increasing gloom outside, I asked him about the Rouge ammo rumor. He said he wouldn't count on it as he had also heard of a large shipment coming from Communist China to help the Rouge finish their little project. Nice! John added that about an hour ago a piece of an incoming rocket punched a hole in the nose of the TIA DC-8.

Another quiet run back to Saigon and we were beginning to wonder if we would get a welcome ho-hum day. Really relaxing was out of the question as Jim and I had been conditioned to not do so until SM Oil was in hand. Dick was sensitive enough to pick up our vibes so his jaw muscles were twitching in time with ours.

Trip number three of the day and once again I held the reins. The funeral gray of water-laden stratus clouds was darkening by the mile and the first traces of moisture were showing as jiggling tiny beads working their way to the top of the windshield. Dick was handling the radios.

"Tailpipe Bravo this is Nancy ... 40 out ... level 15,000."

"Nancy, Tailpipe ... There's a couple of Birds trying to work into November Lima (Neak Luong) under the overcast ... they have a 14,000 altitude cap so shouldn't be a factor for you ... no other significant traffic ... expect 23 ... call 20 out ... we have R minus (light rain) at this time."

"Tailpipe this is Nancy ... understand."

I could feel my pulse rate pick up and Dick's jaw muscle was following right along. Jim called the in-range checklist complete. We were showing 25 miles out and Dick had just picked up his microphone to call 20 when Tailpipe Bravo broke the silence.

"Nancy, Tailpipe." *Now what?*

"Tailpipe this is Nancy ... go ahead."

"Nancy, Tailpipe ... hold at 20 out ... maintain 15,000 ... contact Saigon Control on 125.9 for further ... Tailpipe, out."

"Nancy."

Jim handed up a slip of paper with the best holding speeds for minimum fuel consumption as Dick changed radios.

"Saigon Control this is Tiger 783 ... 25.9 ... go ahead."

Saigon was apparently aware of what was going on (glad somebody was) as they came right back with a clearance.

"Tiger 783, Saigon ... cleared present position direct to Echo then Track 6 to Saigon ... maintain 16,000."

I nudged the power up a bit as I eased Nancy into a climbing left turn. Jim called 15 for 16 (thousand feet) and Dick motioned for me to monitor Saigon while he called the company.

"Tiger operations this is Nancy ... go ahead."

"Nancy, Tiger Ops ... we're ready for you (it was Gary's voice) ... we just got the message that you are returning due to heavy 105 activity ... we'll refuel you and I guess you'll stand by on the ramp ... is that okay?"

"Tiger Ops, Nancy ... roger that's fine ... see you then."

I can still feel the sinking sensation in my gut. Dammit anyway! I'd have given a bunch of something for a modern fighter-bomber with all the trimmings! Other than radio calls none of us said much as we found our way back to Saigon with 96,000 pounds of useless rice.

My approach and landing were normal this time as we had cargo (rice) on board and the brakes were cool. Dick steered us to the ramp and after shutdown Nancy had a drink of kerosene while we opened sandwich wrappers. Jim "borrowed" a navigation radio receiver and tuned in a country-western music station. None of us felt very chatty and for a while the only sounds heard in the cockpit were those made by Loretta Lynn and crinkling waxed paper accented by an occasional "hsst" of a pop can being opened.

Dick settled back in his seat for a nap and Jim was reading a book as I got up to stretch a bit. Though Nancy was first in line to go, Tiger 791 also had a crew standing by so I wandered over to say hello and maybe start a rumor or whatever. I had just said "hi" when their radio came alive with a ten minutes to start warning for Nancy. I said "bye" and as I went out the door heard Jim acknowledge followed by, "791, Nancy ... is Larry over there?" I paused long enough to hear someone say I was on my way then I hurried back across the ramp.

By the time Dick had led us to Neak Luong the weather had really gotten sticky. Dark and wet with even a little bump now and then I found myself worrying about Nancy's name being washed off. We'd been told Phnom Penh hadn't had any action for an hour or so, and especially because it was raining, it was hoped the Rouge were indeed out of ammunition. At least for a while.

There was one "on the other hand" though. That was the possibility they were simply waiting for an airplane to shoot at and we were the first duck in the gallery! My adrenaline pump went from "standby" to "idle."

If misery loves company, we should have been pleased when the radio came alive and Blue 46 announced they were 40 miles out but it just seemed to add to the confusion. Tailpipe advised them we were in the area and asked them to report 20 out.

When we dropped through about 4,000 feet in our steep descent we came out of the clouds into a light but steady drizzle. Visibility looked to be around seven or eight miles. *No problem there; now if the radio will remain without bad news.* We all jumped a bit when Tailpipe tersely cleared us to land "Our discretion!" Hell, if we had even an ounce of discretion between us we'd be a thousand miles away from here!

Dick led Nancy around the Palace and I mentioned I had the TV tower in sight. *No puffs of smoke in town.* Dick called for the landing gear to be lowered. I did that and verified we had three green lights (wheels down and locked). I set full (landing) flaps on command and Jim called the before-landing checklist complete.

We were lined up on final approach and still no sign of trouble. Everything seemed in slow motion. As we crossed over a rain-slickened street I saw a few people walking or riding bicycles. *Wet black umbrellas, and for God's sake! A group of monks in their saffron robes! It looks too normal! This isn't a war zone. No one is starving. Yeah, sure.*

Dick was right on the money as he smoothly raised the nose to transition from descent to gentle landing. He got his gentle landing but it was accompanied by the ugly rattling of shrapnel as we passed through a double cloud of black smoke! Dick didn't waiver a bit as he kept his mind on the job of rolling straight and stopping Nancy in time for the left turn to the ramp. A brown puff just to our left then *"Krack!"* Tailpipe didn't have time to warn any bunnies!

We were on the taxiway facing the ramp when a large cloud of brown smoke appeared right in the offloading area. I said, "Aw shit, someone got hurt by that one!"

Nancy was trapped! Even if we had room to turn around, which we didn't, we couldn't use the short takeoff with our load of rice on board. We all double checked the zippers on our flak jackets and exercised our only option by continuing into the parking area. Blue 46 was back on the radio.

"Tailpipe this is Blue 46 ... 20 out."

"Blue 46, Tailpipe ... we've had some real bad stuff here ... how long can you hold?"

"Tailpipe, Blue 46 ... about 20 minutes ... this is our third try today."

"Blue 46, Tailpipe ... roger we understand but we have Nancy on the ramp and as soon as she is offloaded we want them outta here without delay."

"Tailpipe, Blue 46 ... we'll cancel for today and try again tomorrow."

"Blue 46, Tailpipe ... understand and thank you sir."

After we were parked I looked to the right and spotted the Old Woman. Tears rolled down her lined face as she looked at me and held her apron spread in front of her. I had no trouble spotting the blood and body parts she was trying to hide. I choked as I thought the worst then the Old Man appeared with a bucket of sand to toss on the mess. Thank God! My first thought had been that the Old Woman was guarding his remains.

I saw something squashed into a puddle of blood. It looked like a flattened Flying Tiger baseball cap and whether it was or not, my mind has kept that image to this day.

The score was: Four killed outright, two lost both legs and died on the way to an aid station, and one more died at the aid station. Several others were wounded. Lord Jim and I lost some gentle friends on this fine day. Dick seemed in a bit of a daze as he just sat and quietly stared.

Bad news, good news. The good news was the Rouge shooter didn't put two or three more rounds into the same spot. That probably would have ended the Ricelift along with Nancy and her crew. Two more rockets exploded at Sunnybrook but no more 105mm artillery while we unloaded.

Now short handed, the Cambodian boss quickly recruited several FANK soldiers to push pallets of rice to the door of the airplane. When he had things more or less under control, the visibly disturbed bossman came into the cockpit. His hands were shaking so badly he didn't have to flick the ashes from his cigarette and he had tears wetting his cheeks.

He pointed outside and said: "Look at that silly old woman. She thinks you won't come back if you see a little blood." Then: "When is America gonna help us? We can't do this anymore. We can't live like this anymore. When?!" Tears started to flow faster and embarrassed, he put his head down and turned to leave. He turned around again and staring straight at me said: "When?" Hoping the whole truth wasn't showing on my face I simply said, "They haven't told us yet." He continued to stare for a moment, then he patted me on the shoulder and went back to boss what was left of his crew, of his friends.

When he was gone, Lord Jim turned to me and asked what I meant by: "They haven't told us yet." "It's true," I said. Jim just stared until Dick spoke up and said my answer was about all any of us could have said. Then, thankfully, the radio came to life and changed the subject.

"Tailpipe Bravo this is Tiger 791 ... 40 out ... level 15,000."

"Tiger 791, Tailpipe ... maintain 15,000 ... Phnom Penh airport is closed for the time being ... contact Saigon Control on 125.9 for clearance back to Saigon."

Tailpipe this is Tiger 791 ... Saigon Control on 125.5."

"125.9 for Tiger 791."

"Tiger 791 ... understand ... 125.9 ... Thank you."

You could hear the edge on Tailpipe's radioman's voice. This was not a happy day.

It took a while but we were finally ready to go. Once again, I wished we could just load everybody on board, leave, and never look back. When we started to move out I found the Old Couple and waved. They returned my wave but it was very sad when the usual smiles didn't surface this time.

We were in position on the runway facing northeast when we all felt something. Then, "All bunnies ... incoming! Right behind you Nancy ... cleared for immediate take-off." With all that incentive we didn't hesitate. Dick rolled into the climbing right turn and I was able to look back to my right, easily spotting a ball of black smoke drifting away from the runway.

I had the company radio frequency tuned on one of the radios and when we had gained enough altitude it came to life. We recognized Gary's voice.

"Nancy this is Tiger Ops ... go ahead."

Jim answered, "Yeah Gary this is Nancy."

"Nancy, Tiger Ops ... everything okay?"

"Yeah we're fine but Tailpipe's a mess right now ... We gonna try one more?"

"Yeah Jim, we'll get the load onboard but it'll be iffy ... it's so late you'll have to head right back up ... 791 is just leaving with all the holding fuel they can carry so we'll see how they do ... TIA's through for today with some sheet metal repair ... they'll be the first duck in the gallery tomorrow."

"Nancy ... understand."

"Tiger Ops ... out."

It was now obvious no one was going to set any records today and the hungry were going to get hungrier. Unless you've been there it's almost impossible to imagine the level of our frustration. I suppose this is similar to how firemen would feel if they responded to a house fire with a pumper full of water but their hose wouldn't reach. Just watch it burn and try to ignore the screams.

On the ground at Saigon, Jim monitored the refueling while the loaders quickly gave us another load of rice. Gary had met us as we pulled into the ramp and was now sitting in a jump seat with a microphone in his hand.

Just as we were beginning our rush to get back in the air, Tiger 791 came on the company frequency. Gary answered and we let everything slow to a stop as we heard them say they had been unable to land at PP and were returning (again) with their load.

One of the Tiger Ops people came into the cockpit and said they had just received a message that confirmed PP was closed due to heavy 105mm activity. I hoped tomorrow morning would see an improvement.

Gary got up to leave and said the SM Oil was cold. "See you inside."

After we gathered up our stuff, Grant drove us to the office where we grabbed twosies of SM Oil and retreated to a corner desk. Dick still seemed unruffled by his "interesting" first day of food handling. I mentioned this and he just said it was about what he expected after hearing the war stories floating around the system. He said he had hoped these stories were greatly exaggerated but the opposite seemed to be true. Jim repeated what we had said earlier about this being the worst day yet and added: "I'm afraid we're going to be updating those stories daily from now on."

We mainly just sat quietly in the van and watched traffic on the way to the hotel. Probably because of the gray overcast it was getting dark a lot earlier this late afternoon. "Hey, you got another boss?" Maria greeted us and gave Dick a quick once-over before handing him a paper without even asking if he wanted one. We had briefed him well I guess, he didn't hesitate to cough up the quarter.

Dick had agreed earlier that our Mom and Pop place sounded just right for dinner so after a bit of freshening up we met in the lobby and headed in that direction. After another simple but great meal we wandered around and up and down some side streets just taking in the sights. None of us had even mentioned the nightmare of our last run. I was not too keen on the idea of being alone with the images my mind had stored away. The fact we were going to try again first thing tomorrow morning probably saved me a few bucks worth of rum and later, aspirin.

I'm sure we were all thinking the same as we seemed to be avoiding the hotel but being tired (again) we reluctantly headed back and after lingering in the lobby for a while went to our rooms.

As I passed CBS, a photojournalist spotted me, came out into the hallway and asked me about what had happened. He had heard something about bad things but no details. I gave him a quick recap and when I mentioned the Cambodian boss and his question about someone helping them he said I should scream bloody murder when I get home. I said: "You send stuff like this all the time don't you?" He said: "Yeah but it gets changed a bit between here and there." "You mean they fake things?" He answered not really, but just the other day some of his stuff was aired on the evening news in the States.

The powers that be had taken clips from two of his tapes and combined them into one short piece. What people saw on their TVs was a peasant woman crying her eyes out while holding the bloody, dead body of her small child out to the camera (his). The picture then smoothly switched to a South Vietnamese tank with its crew smiling and waving! "Did they say the South Vietnamese had killed the kid?" I asked. "No, but they didn't say they hadn't. What would you think if you saw that?"

He went on, "I took the tape of that tank over three weeks ago during a training exercise and the woman with her child just four days ago. The child was killed by NVA artillery!"

His eyes were a little bleary and I was getting a buzz from his breath so I could tell he would probably sleep tonight. He shook my hand and I was sure he was thinking, "Welcome to the Club."

Good night Sir.

22 March 1975

South Vietnam: The Convoy of Tears, under constant attack and blocked by the Ba River, resumes moving toward the coast after a temporary bridge is built. The wounded, ill, and starving refugees having suffered drought and relentless heat are now subjected to a steady cold rain. More refugees are falling by the wayside and many are giving up the road to take their chances in the jungle.

What a night! Tossing and turning, then lying quietly listening to "bumps," then slipping into a light sleep. Wake up, turn over the now sweat-soaked pillow, and toss and turn some more. I didn't have any dreams with vivid images but whatever was running around in my head was very unpleasant. It didn't make me feel one bit better to know there were a few zillion people close by that would gladly trade places with me.

For once it was a relief when my phone hummed at 5 AM.

The hot shower felt good. Thank God for clean, plentiful hot water and American TP! I could put up with almost anything as long as I had those two things. Hiram provided a little touch of comfort by distracting my thoughts for a fleeting moment. Then it was get dressed, move past the rhythmic rattle of the newsroom teletypes, and go down the stairs to the lobby for the 21st time in a row.

We stopped at Steve's Place even though none of us really had an appetite. Dick and I just settled for coffee and rolls. Jim ordered a breakfast but only ate a little. *I could hear my Mother's voice, "Don't waste that! There are children starving in China you know."*

The order in the gallery that morning was TIA's DC-8 first, then Tiger 791, and finally it would be our turn. TIA was due to land at PP

163

soon so the 791 crew went to their airplane while we dawdled in the office for a few minutes and sipped some more coffee.

It was another cloudy day with spotty rain falling all over Southeast Asia. Not good.

The van dropped us off in front of Nancy just as 791 rumbled down the runway and lifted off into a flat, gray sky. Jim had completed his preflight inspection. He had everything set up and ready to go, so Dick and I didn't have much to do other than stow our flight kits and sit down.

I missed the usual good-natured banter we would throw at each other at the beginning of a flight but the images of yesterday plus the apprehension of what today might have in store really threw everyone's mood into the basement. We just waited, mostly in silence.

Grant came aboard and after quietly saying something about the tires, just wrote some notes in the logbook and went outside again.

The company radio came alive.

"Tiger Ops this is Tiger 791 ... go ahead."

This got our attention as they hadn't had time to even land in PP yet, let alone be on their way back. Now what!

We recognized Gary's voice: "Tiger 791 this is Ops ... go ahead."

"Tiger Ops, Tiger 791 ... we'll be landing (at) Saigon in about ah ... 25 minutes ... unable (to land at) PP."

"791, ops ... understand ... break ... Nancy, Ops ... you copy that?"

"Ops, Nancy ... roger."

"Nancy, Ops ... standby ... I'll be out shortly."

Grant was standing on my side of the airplane talking to a couple of his guys. I reached out and slapped the side hard enough for him to hear it over the noise of the running ground equipment and when he looked my way I motioned for him to come up to the cockpit. He misread though and got on the intercom instead. "You guys ready? I thought we had about 20 minutes to go yet." I picked up the mike and told him about 791 and he said he'd be right up. He was on his way when Gary arrived in the van. Gary got out and said something to Grant, then led the way as they both came up to the cockpit. Grant ran his finger across his throat and after we shut down our navigation computers and some other equipment he had someone on the ground shut down the noisy generator.

Gary broke the ensuing silence by informing us he had received a landline (telephone) message that the TIA DC-8 and a Bird C-130 were both seriously damaged on the ramp at PP and the TIA DC-8 was burning! That was all he knew at the moment. We would all stand by until more details came in. We went through the parking checklist (no important switches left on, etc.) and leaving our kits on board we climbed into the van. Grim faced, Gary drove us to the office.

The crew of 791 came in and they were just as ignorant as we were. About three un-needed cups of black coffee later I decided to walk back to the airplane simply for something to do that might keep my mind off this latest bit of unpleasant information.

Approaching Nancy, I noticed Col. C. sitting in his idling Jeep near Nancy's boarding stand. As I walked up to him he kind of waved and I wondered about the silly little smile he was showing. I caught a movement in the doorway of the airplane and curious, I went up the stand. Col. C. still hadn't said a word.

When I looked into the cockpit I saw someone dressed in a khaki uniform leaning over the captain's seat apparently rummaging through Dick's flight kit. I could feel a slow burn coming on as I said: "Can I help you with something?" This person stood and turned to face me. The Polish General! The "Communist" Polish General in charge of the ICCS (International Commission of Control and Supervision)!

"What in hell do you think you're doing?" I asked. He said: " I am inspecting this airplane." When I asked him "for what?" he said he was simply checking to make sure we weren't smuggling arms into Cambodia. Feeling blood rushing to my face I said, as calmly as I could: "Cambodia is none of your business!" He said he was making it his business, then he made a mistake that could have (should have?) cost him his life. He turned his back to me and reached for my flight kit. Now there was nothing in my kit that would have interested him and I could have just let him play his game while I calmly stood there and watched but he had pushed a button.

Days of extreme frustration surfaced. Days of being shot at by an unseen (communist) enemy. Days of hearing of or seeing people hurt and killed by these unseen "things" and now I was looking at one! I must have made a sound of some kind as he straightened a bit when I lunged for him. The first thing I saw that might be handy was the epaulet on his right shoulder. I grabbed that and yanked with more than all my strength! I felt the button pop loose as I twisted to my left and sent him sailing out of the cockpit where he crashed back-first into the crew galley. The coffee jug spigot was unlocked and it spewed hot dark liquid down the back of his shirt. I stepped on his hat as I went after him again. At the doorway he paused, probably alarmed at the thought of quickly going down such a steep stairway, and I prepared to kick him as hard as I could in the small of his back!

Call it what you may, civilization? Conditioning? I doubt it was divine intervention but something stopped me! I just couldn't give that probably fatal last kick. He almost did it for me as he scrambled down the stand and nearly fell as he tripped twice. I sailed his hat like a frisbee and when it hit the ground it rolled past Col. C. My target quickly retrieved it and jumped into the jeep. I think Col. C. was going to get verbal with me as he didn't drive away but this just gave me another shot at the General.

I was so bloody mad I was literally seeing red! I asked: "What the fuck is going on C?" He answered: "Partridge, this man is a General!" I said: "A fucking communist General, you idiot. He ranks below the lowest private in the South Vietnamese Army!"

I suppose I should have guessed what C. would come up with next: "He speaks English so watch your words young man." I said: "Good, now listen carefully, both of you." The General just sat red faced while staring straight ahead. "Colonel, if I ever catch this thing even looking at my airplane again I will gladly break his fucking neck! Do you understand?" They both just stared straight ahead. The General had a small pistol in a patent leather holster and I found myself hoping he'd make some kind of move toward it. "Do you understand?" They both nodded. " Good, now Colonel get this worthless pile of dogshit out of my sight before I do it now!"

Col. C. let the clutch out too fast and his Jeep just jumped once and died. The General's hat ended up in the back and they probably suffered a bit of whiplash. I would have laughed but I was so far over the hill with anger I was about to puke! Col. C. finally got things in order and away they went.

I turned around and almost bumped into a South Vietnamese Army Captain with an MP (military police) armband and a Colt .45 pistol hanging from his belt. I was about to say "Now what the fuck do you want," when he offered me his hand. He was a slight chap but his handshake was strong as he smiled and clapped me on the arm with his left hand. He then stepped back, saluted me, and returned to his Jeep, still smiling.

I was glad none of my own people had seen my little show. It was all so out of control and probably dumb but I really couldn't help myself once that jerk pushed me over the line.

I took off at a fast walk down the taxiway. Now that no one could see me I started spilling stupid tears! *Now I see why so many people are doing this. It feels kind of good! Maybe it's how your body gets rid of excess adrenaline.* I calmed quite a bit as I "let it go."

I was unwinding nicely and my pace had slowed somewhat when I heard the distinct sound of a C-130 coming up behind me. As I turned to watch this VNAF machine go by on its way to takeoff, I was shocked to see the right wingtip was badly damaged. I held my arms up and crossing my forearms slowly clenched my fists. This is a universal signal for stopping an aircraft. They came to a stop beside me and when I pointed to the damaged area the co-pilot nodded to inform me they knew about it then they continued on to the departure runway.

Silly me! Had I forgotten there was a war going on? I would have given anything to wake up at home and find this whole adventure had been just a very elaborate and realistic dream.

Under control, I started back to where Nancy was parked. I thought about the consequences of my losing it with the Polish General and what Col. C. must be screaming at Gary right now. I looked up the taxiway to our ramp area almost expecting to see flashing red lights and troops with dogs searching for the berserk killer on the loose, me. All was calm and as I approached our ramp I could see Grant and a Vietnamese mechanic tinkering with a piece of loading equipment.

Grant noticed me and with his wide smile asked if it was true I had just declared war on Poland. He said a Vietnamese MP stopped by and gave a blow by blow account of my show. I told Grant the whole story and finished by wondering if a pot of oil was being heated for my benefit. He confirmed my earlier thought that the ICCS had "zero" authority over anything civilian or Cambodian and what I had said about it being none of the General's business was absolutely true! "Why didn't you kick his ass off the stand?" Grant asked. I answered: "Paperwork, Grant. You know how pilots hate paperwork and that would have caused a bunch!"

"He was put here just to oversee the cease-fire?" I went on, "If so, why isn't he gone, now that the cease-fire is history?" Grant said apparently the guy hadn't been officially recalled yet and was no doubt reluctant to end this "paid vacation" for him and his family. I said: "Vacation? In a war zone?" Grant's answer was to say that almost anywhere beats being in communist Poland, war or no war. Good point!

Then Grant made me feel even better by saying all the people including flight crews at PP were okay. The TIA DC-8 crew had gone into the Tailpipe bunker when the shelling had become intense but when their airplane started burning they reboarded and moved it to a spot where it wouldn't block the ramp. They then shut her down completely and returned to the bunker joining the Bird C-130 crew who had also moved their aircraft out of the way after it was badly damaged. If medals were handed out to civilian crews these guys had earned a handful! The lonely crew of the old fire truck at PP also risked their butts by staying on the job and successfully snuffing the fire on and under the right wing of the TIA DC-8.

While we were chatting we saw the company van stop in front of 791. After her crew got off, Gary drove up to us and stopped to let Dick and Jim out. Gary said everyone was calling it a day so when we retrieved our stuff from the cockpit he would take us to the office.

After climbing into the front passenger seat with my flight kit I asked Gary if he had talked to Col. C. in the last hour or so. He gave me an apprehensive glance and asked: "You haven't been messing with him again have you?" I said: "I guess not" and Gary just said he didn't want to hear about it. Then he shook his head and muttered: "I guess not!" It was obvious Gary hadn't been told anything so I relaxed even further.

Actually, I never did hear a peep about what had taken place that morning. I could assume I was well within my rights by giving the good General a taste of my "respect" for him. What puzzles me to this day is why Col. C. cooperated so completely with the slimeball.

On the way to the hotel someone mentioned there was an interesting Vietnamese restaurant we should try. It was on a barge moored on the Saigon River and served excellent seafood. A bit expensive but worth it. Dick said he'd go if we did. I was all for it but Jim just said he'd think about it. Dick said he would have the desk at the hotel make reservations for the two of us and if Jim decided to go there would still be two empty seats at our table. No problem. Great! I was finally going to get the good seafood dinner I missed in Bangkok.

For lunch we ended up at Steve's for burgers, fries, and cold beer. After we arrived back at the hotel, I felt the effects of my lousy night's sleep and excused myself to head for my room. Dick said he'd give me a wake-up call. I thanked him and headed up the stairs. I managed to struggle through yesterday's (simple) crossword then slipped into a deep sleep, traffic noise and all.

I was kind of awake and trying to organize my thoughts when the phone hummed. It was Dick calling to wake me. We had our reservations at the floating restaurant okay but the only opening was a little early. This was Saturday, their busiest day, and I guess we were lucky to get aboard at all. Dick had tried Jim's room but no answer. He did come up with two more people to join us. I said I'd go rinse and spit and meet them in the lobby after a bit.

After I put down the phone, I peeked outside and saw the weather had improved a lot. Everything was bathed in the warm golden glow of a late afternoon sun.

Downstairs, I chatted with Maria while cabs were being rounded up. I paid my bill to date and she said she'd put today's paper in my mailbox. Then she asked: "Who's the lady seein' Jim?" Now it was my turn to say: "Is she pretty?" "Yeah, I think so." Then a little jealousy showed. "They went out and he didn' see me at all! He likes her a lot?" I said they were good friends and the lady works for a newspaper, like Maria. I also told her he and I were really tired lately and that's probably the reason he missed seeing her. "I said you guys work too much. That's not good, you know." Then I told her we would be going home soon and we'd get lots of rest then. "I'm never gonna see you again?" I assured her we'd be back real soon.

Two cabs were easy to come by but we were having trouble finding any more. One of the drivers reminded us it was Saturday and they were very busy. They didn't like sitting and waiting for us so we settled for two. I think this pleased Maria as she gave a little wave along with one of her rare smiles. I didn't know this would be the last time I'd see her … ever.

The cabs took us southeast all the way down Tu Do Street to the Saigon River, then a slight turn to the right and we had arrived. Buildings had been razed along the edge of the river to create a clear zone that would expose any intruders trying to move from the river into the city. It also exposed a straggling line of nicely dressed diners picking their way around rubble and trying to keep from stepping in puddles while getting to the barge.

As if that scene wasn't strange enough, the tide was out and one corner of the restaurant was hard aground, tilting the whole works a few degrees away from shore. As we were led to our table we noticed well-armed and camouflaged sentries all up and down the shoreline.

It was very clear that a war was in progress but people, being the strange and flexible creatures they are, will try their damnedest to ignore the obvious and grimly hang onto what they have always done and enjoyed. After all, it was Saturday night wasn't it?

We all felt like we had finished our first drink already because of the subtle tilt of the floor (deck?). There was a small dance floor and

WWII big band music was playing but no one seemed up to the challenge of dancing on a hillside. Drinks were slow to arrive and we imagined that too was because of the slanted bar and tables.

This gave us time to examine our surroundings. The barge was huge, maybe 150 feet long by 75 wide. The kitchen/bar area was on one end and the rest was open-air dining and dancing. Tables were covered with white linen and lighting was mainly furnished by paper lanterns hanging every ten feet or so above the main area. Perhaps it was because we were so far above the water but we gratefully noticed a lack of mosquitos.

The tide was now definitely rising and our round of drinks arrived to rest on an almost level table. We ordered our dinners and my choice was a whole cracked crab smothered in hot chili sauce. The waiter said it would be a while so please relax and enjoy ourselves. We leaned back and did just that.

The incoming tide brought more than just a level dance floor. It was a scene so rich in visual and emotional impact that professional movie makers would have sold their soul to receive credit for creating it.

On glassy, calm water and bathed in the burnt orange glow of a spectacular sunset, three boats came around a bend of the river downstream and headed slowly toward us. Two of them were painted a light gray with white numbers on the side, obviously navy and about the size of Jacques Cousteau's miniship, the *Calypso*. The other was smaller and appeared to be some kind of fishing vessel. They all had a strange silhouette, a sort of out-of-focus look. Then, about the same time the throb of their diesel engines could be heard, their strange appearance was explained. All three boats were absolutely packed with people! There was not a square inch of space that was not touched by a human in some way.

I was relieved when someone had the sensitivity and sense to shut off the tape deck that was somewhat loudly playing Glenn Miller's "In the Mood."

The staff and patrons of the restaurant neither moved nor spoke as this very sad and tragic parade slowly and carefully moved past to a moorage somewhere upstream. They had no doubt come from Danang, a trip of about 500 miles that would have taken at least 24 hours in open seas! As the boats moved out of sight the sun also dipped below the horizon and it rapidly became dark.

At first I wanted to leave, but then I realized everyone here knew what they were doing. They weren't callously ignoring the situation.

They and we were all actors going through the final act of some sort of play. Everyone knew this would all be gone, if not tomorrow then the next day or whatever. This was a farewell party! A last salute to "the good life" and it would be yet another tragedy if we all went home and let this old barge die in silence.

I knew my thoughts were universal when everyone returned to life and began the celebration. Crying and laughing or laughing and crying, who cares? It was good to see the previously uptight crowd come alive and really enjoy their "last supper."

Our food finally arrived and it looked great! My crab was a huge dark red guy with beautiful black tips on his claws. The meat was sweet, rich and done just right with a sauce that was really hot but also had lots of flavor. Excellent! We washed everything down with, what else ... schooners of draft beer that rivaled anything I'd had in Germany. Now if I could only erase the images of the boat people staring back at us.

We finally gave up our table to the next in line and made our way through "no man's land" to the street and the line of cabs. While waiting for two of them to drive up to us we noticed the ever-present flashes to the northwest and a drop of three flares just a couple miles away down the river. It was hard to believe we were that close to a probably mortal conflict, especially when we rode back up Tu Do Street and saw lots of people shopping or just walking around enjoying the warm Saturday evening.

Back at the hotel I said my good nights and wandered up the stairs to my room. All was quiet except for the usual teletype chatter so I didn't have to make any decisions about attending or passing up a debriefing. In my room I poured myself a tall, weak nightcap and sat by the window. Flash then bump then girlish laughter from the street below. I wondered if I ever would get my head back on straight when this was behind me.

My lids got a little heavy so, leaving the shade open, I laid on the bed and listened to noises while watching the play of neon colors and traffic lights on the ceiling. It all soon faded.

Good night Saigon.

23 March 1975

South Vietnam: The city of Hue is now surrounded and cut off from the rest of Vietnam except by sea. The last few Americans in Hue are evacuated by helicopter to Danang.

I awoke to the silence of the curfew at 2 AM and did the "don't step on Hiram" shuffle to the bathroom and back to bed. Once again I had a feeling that I hated, absolutely dead tired but wide awake! I let my mind wander.

The sad but somehow beautiful spectacle of the refugee-packed boats on the river was vividly rerun by my imagination. What would happen to other boat people if the weather decided to get nasty?

I thought about Maria attending Mass in the morning and the comfort she and others must be enjoying by having at least that age-old ritual to rely upon. I envied her.

My mind rambled on.

I wondered how my family was getting along. If I miss them so much, why am I almost afraid to go home. Am I not "me" anymore? How could I change so much in just three weeks? My wife must be about ready for the "loony bin" after spending so much time alone with three young tigers (sons). Then I thought, being married to a pilot she just might be used to working alone. Now I could go off on a little guilt trip while I tried to get sleepy.

Memory of my wonderful dinner slowly faded then I was rudely brought back to life by traffic noises and gray daylight. I thought curfew had just ended but a look at my watch told me it was almost 10 AM! Obviously I had slept, but not with quality. I had a gritty edge and my neck was stiff.

I called the office and after a short wait Gary came on the line. He said Phnom Penh was still closed. The DC-8 and C-130 were still there but ground crews from U Tapao were working on them and should have them out by this evening. We talked about how neat it was that both aircraft would fly away from the mess at PP, provided, of course, the Rouge didn't nail them again. A lot of airline passengers would be happy to know just how much punishment airplanes can take and still function.

Gary then told me two pilots were on their way to relieve Jim and me. We could plan on flying tomorrow if PP was open and we'd probably be leaving for home sometime on Tuesday if any flights out of Saigon were available. After I said I'd pass this on to Jim we hung up.

I felt it again. Panic was too strong a term, but close to what I felt when I thought of leaving.

I tried Jim's room and wonder of wonders, he answered! I passed on the news and we agreed to meet in the lobby after which we would press on to Mom and Pop's place for lunch.

On my way to meet Jim, I peeked into the newsroom. Seeing no sign of Peter, I wondered if he was out pulling strings to get his in-laws out of Danang. The few people in the office seemed busy so I continued on to the lobby, probably a little early. Jim must have been hungry as he was standing just outside the entry when I spotted him.

We wasted no time on our way to the cafe, and as it was Sunday, had no trouble getting a table. We both ordered omelets and were pleased we no longer had to ask for the tiny bottle of Tabasco sauce. The proprietor (and chef) even smiled while he looked down his nose at our "rude alteration" of his culinary creation. At least we didn't ask for ketchup. We properly and honestly praised his efforts and he widened his smile to show a glint of gold.

We never had anything but wonderful food when we chose this little cafe. I wonder what ever became of them. They (Mom and Pop) seemed a bit old to start over in some new and strange place.

When Jim and I talked about going home, I mentioned my strange reaction to the thought. Jim was surprised to find he wasn't alone in feeling this way. He didn't understand it either but he agreed it was very real. "Maybe we're just having too much fun," he said. Using Maria's favorite two-word answer I said: "Yeah, sure."

After we sipped the last of our delicious coffee we said *merci beaucoup, au revoir* and without even thinking this may be our last meal at this homey little place (it was), we headed out for a long walk around the area.

In some places you had to go into the street to get around sidewalk vendors who had their wares covering the entire sidewalk. Anything one could possibly imagine was for sale, from sewing needles to heavy-duty tools. Chewing gum to cigarettes to tee shirts and caged birds. Even some airplane parts and empty brass artillery shells that would be melted down and recast as ship's bells or candlesticks. Even giant economy-size boxes of US-made laundry detergent. It didn't take too much imagination to realize a lot of this stuff was acquired for way less than wholesale. Especially when some of it would magically disappear when an MP would pass by, and in the blink of an eye, reappear when he was out of sight.

Mostly legitimate and some not. From Mom and Pop's cafe and Steve's Place to stolen soap, this city was wall-to-wall free enterprise … the commies were going to hate it!

We wandered past our hotel and stopped for a beer at the large open-air "Maxim's" style cafe at the base of the Continental Palace Hotel. I guess we had a lot to think about as we didn't talk much. It was mostly watching for ladies wearing the Ao Dai while we nursed a couple of beers.

Tiring of that, we continued on up Tu Do Street and when we came to the "Bunny Club" Jim put on his mean little smile and suggested, just for old time's sake, we both go in and shout "All Bunnies, Incoming!" He must have been a bit tired as I easily talked him out of it. I told him it would be really neat to be blown away by a nervous bouncer after surviving 50 missions to Phnom Penh.

We walked around the American Embassy and turned down the wide tree-lined boulevard that ran parallel to and just northeast of Tu Do Street.

When we came to Brink's Hotel we went up to their restaurant and checked the Sunday buffet dinner menu. Tex-Mex night sounded good so we decided to come back around 6 PM and give it a try.

Jim and I completed the loop by passing the old French Opera House and ending up back at The Caravelle. Once again, the thought never occurred to us that we were seeing all this for the last time … ever.

We were disappointed and curious when Maria was nowhere to be seen. Thinking we had missed her, we went to the hotel desk to check our mail boxes but no newspaper. Strange.

We had some time to kill before dinner so while Jim went to his room to lie down for a while, I wandered up to the newsroom. Peter still wasn't around but a correspondent, Eric Cavaliero, spotted me and reminded me that I had promised him a look at the notes I was keeping. I went to my room and retrieved them. I was going to rewrite everything to eliminate the politically incorrect passages (mostly about Col. C.) in Eric's copy but I had forgotten all about it. After Eric assured me he wouldn't use the stuff I had marked, I just let him borrow the original. I figured I was leaving soon anyway so what the hell. It turned out I had nothing to worry about, Eric didn't touch any of the bad stuff.

We chatted for a while and then I retreated to my room. An envelope had been slipped under the door and the message it contained was from Tigers. The TIA DC-8 was back in U Tapao and the C-130 was expected out of PP before dark. We could expect the good old 5 AM wake-up call. Also, reservations had been made for Jim and me on China Airlines to Hong Kong, leaving Saigon at 10 AM on Tuesday.

I had a double lump in my throat. A big one for the family I would be coming home to and one only a little smaller for the family I would be leaving behind. In spite of the plans and promises, I had a strong feeling I would not be returning. Ever.

Jim called when he woke from his nap and we met in the bar for a little before-dinner toddy. That taken care of, we looked around for Maria. Having no luck at that, we went on to Brink's and proceeded to pig out on a "not too shabby" Tex-Mex dinner. Things weren't nearly as spicy as I like but it was quite good. Right down to, and including, the flan.

When we returned to the hotel we asked the desk clerk about Maria. He said before we moved in, Maria often went missing for a day or two but this was the first day in the last three weeks she had missed. We thanked him and went back outside for a last look. Even her little helpers were conspicuously absent. We hoped she'd be at her post tomorrow afternoon. It definitely wouldn't be right for us to leave without saying good-bye.

We said our "see ya in the mornings" and headed for our rooms, hopefully, to sleep.

The news room was still mostly unoccupied and I wondered if I was going to miss saying good-bye to that gang as well as Maria. I continued on to my room and after noting even Hiram wasn't available for conversation, I sat in the dark and looked and listened out the always-open window.

The swell and fade of various motors and human chatter mixed with occasional laughter lulled my senses. Like staring at lit candles I even found some comfort in the sight of the air-dropped flares that now crowded the sky around the city. Then came the flashes and thumps that reminded me of the tragedy that, like a flooding river, was slowly but surely rising to lay waste the people of Phnom Penh and South Vietnam.

Leaving the drapes open I laid on the bed for a while and watched the flickering lights reflecting on the ceiling. After a tiny burp tasting pleasantly of onion and cumin I slipped into a (mostly) dream-free sleep.

Buenas noches, Hiram.

24 March 1975

South Vietnam: At precisely 6 PM the order to abandon the ancient imperial capital city of Hue is given. Approximately 50,000 people (civilians and troops) make their way east to the coast hoping for rescue by sea. The NVA artillery is redirected and now shells fall into the columns of refugees instead of the city. Less than 8,000 are successfully evacuated.

The wake-up call was a bit late this AM. I didn't have a chance to enjoy any extra sleep though, as I had been awake for a while when the phone hummed. After I hung up, I wondered if the next guest to use "my" room would complain about the lack of a gawd-awful bell ringing in his ear. How quickly your tracks fill in when walking through the soft mud of the world.

None of us were particularly hungry so we skipped Steve's Place and headed nonstop to the airport for donuts, coffee, and whatever else might be interesting. Gary must have been a frustrated mother robin in another life. He always had plenty of goodies stowed on the airplane for us starving birdmen.

The first news of the day wasn't pleasant. An old beater of a C-47 (DC-3) carrying fuel oil into Phnom Penh was approaching to land this morning when they were hit by a SAM-7 missile. Without a peep on the radio, they turned into a ball of fire and plunged into the ground a few miles west of the airport. As this was in Khmer Rouge territory there was no way to check, but it was assumed all four souls on board had returned to earth for the last time. Witnesses said it made a spectacular fire topped by a mile-high column of smoke that lasted for about 45 minutes. So long, guys.

Soon, we were on our way into the shooting gallery. It was only slightly comforting to think about the one important advantage we had over the C-47 crew. Not having the excess horsepower we enjoyed, they had to plod along at a fairly low altitude while hoping they didn't present a very interesting or important target. As you know, we came sliding in at 15,000 feet and spiralled steeply down for our landing. If we did take a bad hit, at least our remains would end up in friendly territory.

I washed a mouthful of chocolate éclair down with a slug of milk and got on the horn (radio) to Tailpipe.

"Tailpipe this is Nancy … 20 out … one five thousand (15,000 feet) … go ahead."

"Nancy, Tailpipe … descend and land your discretion … runway 05 in use … incoming rare so far … traffic is a Bird inbound."

On our way to line-up on runway 05 we looked to the west but saw no obvious sign of where the C-47 had gone in. After we landed and turned around at the east end, we paused to allow the Bird C-130 to land facing us.

When it was certain they were safely down, we taxied west on the runway. As we approached each other head on they came to their turnoff and exited the runway to our left. Then they turned to the west to parallel our track and we could see their load forming on the ramp as they pushed it out of their large rear-facing cargo doors. We made our left turn and as we pulled into the DC-8 parking area the C-130 moved past us and went out to the runway. Facing east, they quickly brought up the power and were on their way back to U Tapao. I wasn't sure what to call the dance we had just done. Waltz … or ballet? Square?

Our Cambodian boss had a full crew again. Several FANK soldiers had volunteered to leave the relative safety of the bunkers and learn how to unload DC-8s. Everything seemed to click and we were back to the speedy offloads.

"All bunnies … incoming." Then a large "Thump" signalled more plowing going on at Sunnybrook Farm as we turned and headed for the runway. Very quickly we were airborne and once again leaving one raging storm for the deceptively quiet "eye" of another.

Just two more trips completed without mishap would mean Lord Jim and I were done. Fifty-three "missions" completed without a scratch.

No more "Thumps" followed by the harsh rattle of metallic hail. No longer would we have the "pleasure" of learning what fresh human blood smelled like on a hot day.

If we were lucky, we could stop trying to think of some way to help the thousands of gentle people in two nations who were strangling on the putrid fumes generated by the fallout of battles between so-called left and right. People choking on the stink of a small piece of shit called Pol Pot who had the notion he could redo his country and its people as if he were a barber trying a new style, but it wasn't hair falling to the floor, it was minds and flesh ... and bones ... acres of bones.

Pol Pot was infected by the same virus Adolf Hitler had sniffed. The most outstanding symptom was the overpowering desire to be the God of this world, no matter what the cost in lives painfully ended. Pot and Adolf overlooked one detail—the job had been filled for a long, long time by a spirit that created as well as destroyed.

Yes, I was in a very somber mood on this, our last (one way or another) day. Jim and I used to drive everyone around us nuts with our constant banter and silly puns but now we seldom spoke at all except for the necessary stuff. Nothing was funny anymore and we knew what each other thought about the serious things. Some may have wondered if we had ceased being friends but actually we had grown so close we were like some twins. No need to talk as you know what the other is thinking.

The approach and landing at Saigon were totally routine but Jim and I felt the building tension of wondering if we were really going to complete our last mission without incident.

Our load was almost complete and the van carrying Tailpipe's lunch was nowhere in sight. The possibility of leaving without it ran against the grain but things were relatively quiet in Phnom Penh. It didn't seem right to ignore that in favor of someone's meal.

We were spared the pain of this decision when the van pulled up with a minute to spare. Lord Jim and I were not cheated out of our last pleasurable sniff of ten hot Steve's Place cheeseburgers and fries. This time, they were all neatly packed in a large box that had seen better days as a container of "Trout" brand Washington State Red Delicious apples.

It was my turn to drive and Dick called out critical speeds as we accelerated down Saigon's runway 25 Left and once again saved wear and tear on the tires by becoming airborne.

Nancy soon had us level at 15,000 feet and on our way. Passing Neak Luong we noted a Bird C-130 preparing to drop a load into a city that (we know now) had exactly one week to live, literally.

Dick called Tailpipe.

"Tailpipe this is Nancy … level 15 … 20 out … go ahead."

"Nancy, Tailpipe … descend and land your discretion … active is (runway) 05 … traffic is Blue 46 inbound, you'll both be here about the same time so maybe you can work together on landing sequence … incoming is still pretty quiet."

"Tailpipe, Nancy … understand."

I steered Nancy toward the Royal Palace then entered a fairly steep turn to the left and rolled out on a heading that took us westbound, parallel to the runway.

Just as we levelled, Dick spotted Blue 46 to our left. As we passed in front of him the radio came alive.

"Nancy this is Blue 46, over."

"Blue 46, Nancy … go ahead."

"Roger … we can turn inside you and land about halfway down the runway … we should be off just as you touch down … would that be okay?"

Dick looked at me and I said: "Sure, that looks good, I'll slow as much as I can and we should have plenty of room."

"Blue 46, Nancy … that sounds okay … we'll slow a bit and you should be right in the slot."

"Nancy this is Blue 46 … Thanks."

When we were about halfway through our right turn to line up with the runway we saw Blue 46 just rolling out and lining up to land ahead of us. The spacing wasn't generous but looked to be okay. Now we were lined up and I double-checked our speed to be sure we were as slow as safely possible. We did the last of the checklist.

Blue 46 showed a puff of blue tire smoke as she touched down. The timing looked perfect, they would be turning off to their ramp well before we passed that spot.

Then the day turned bad. Really bad. Blue 46 was rolling nicely toward their turnoff point and we had just touched down when a large blast of brown smoke erupted just in front of their number one (left) engine and beside the cockpit. Blue 46 began a slow turn to the left and ended up in a cloud of dust facing 90° away from the runway. We lost sight of them as we rolled past. Aw crap … no!

"Nancy, Tailpipe … you clear okay?"

"This is Nancy … yeah we're clear … this does not look good … you got someone to come out and check?"

"Roger … Blue 46, Tailpipe."

"Blue 46, Tailpipe … go ahead."

"Blue 46, Tailpipe." *Come on Blue 46, answer!*

Now we were turned around and I was working the radio: "Tailpipe this is Nancy ... both of their engines are shut down and we don't see any sign of a fire but the doors are still closed and there's no activity. We think someone might be hurt ... bad."

Dick was thinking ahead as he was taxiing a lot faster than normal but in my near state of shock, I didn't notice. I spotted two jeep loads of people just sitting by the bunker, and not thinking at all, I came out with: "Godammit! You got someone coming or what?"

Tailpipe responded by advising me: "Just as soon as you're out of the fucking way our people will go!" Then I remembered. The shortest mine-free way to the runway and Blue 46 was the taxiway we were coming in on. There was no response when I simply said: "Sorry."

When we were at the ramp the Cambodian boss man came into the cockpit and tried to say something but he finally gave up and after giving us each a pat on the shoulder he quietly left. I didn't realize it then but that was the last time I was to see him ... ever.

The Old Couple looked up at us and clasping their hands in front of their faces they bowed ever so slightly then looked up again. The Old Woman had somehow found more large tears to shed. This would be the last time I would see them ... ever.

Later we compared notes and it was unanimous we all felt we would very likely have been in Blue 46's place had they not asked to go ahead of us, thus slowing us down. Another sobering thought was the fact that, due to their relatively slow speed, they hadn't flown even half as many missions as we had in the same period of time.

They enjoyed better odds but still drew the short straw.

As we left, we saw an Air America helicopter had landed beside Blue 46. Doors had been opened and people were moving around the airplane. We knew then that if necessary, Blue 46s crew would soon be in Saigon for medical attention.

We had just signed off with Tailpipe when Gary's voice came up on the radio. "Nancy, Tiger Ops ... go ahead." I answered and the next words from Saigon were: "You guys are through for the day. PP is shutting down for a while to give the fighters a chance to find some targets. Captain Riemer, your new crew will be here soon. Larry and Jim, you two are fired! See you all on the ground."

After I acknowleged, Dick graciously turned the controls over to me and said: "Enjoy it, this will be your last landing in Saigon." Talk about mixed emotions. Relief! ... Guilt? ... Happy ... Sad? ... Sad! ... Peaceful? ... Angry!

Nancy probably gave me a little help but I swear, my final landing in South Vietnam was about the prettiest one I've ever done. Too bad I didn't have a load of passengers to strut in front of after we parked.

Damn, it felt strange to gather up my stuff and prepare to leave my job here. I looked at Jim and reworded my thoughts as leaving *our* job here. I tried to console myself by reminding myself we had really pushed our luck. Fifty-two times on the bull's-eye was enough. We hadn't accomplished as much as we wanted, but by God, we did give it one hell of a try.

Maybe our efforts slowed the KR just enough to allow someone to get out from under the executioner's axe.

It was time to go home.

I put my kit in the back of the van and stood for a long minute just staring back at Nancy. My back was to everyone as I silently mouthed: "Take care girl. I'll see you later, okay? Thanks." Then I turned and climbed into the van. Swallowing hard, I was grateful no one else seemed to feel like talking at the moment. I didn't look back.

Gary met us at the office and filled us in on the story of Blue 46. Shrapnel had bounced off the pavement and punched holes in the lower left side of the cockpit. A large piece entered just below the Captain's ribcage and after doing grievous damage exited just below his right shoulder. Amazingly, he was still alive. The co-pilot had less severe but painful wounds to his left neck area. Both were on their way via Air America helicopter to a hospital in the Saigon area. The airplane was still flyable and a crew were on their way to take it out of PP.

Although we knew little about them other than they were Chinese and spoke excellent English, we felt they were old friends and we prayed silently for them.

Gary handed me a cover letter that told who we were, etc., to be presented to the China Airlines agent. This would get Jim and me on the flight to Hong Kong. We would stay overnight there, then fly the next morning to Tokyo and on to Anchorage, Alaska. Another quick rest, then home.

That taken care of, we stuffed some SM Oil into our kits, said: "See you later" to Gary and others that gathered around, and got back into the van for our last ride to the Caravelle Hotel.

I had so much going through my head the trip was just a blur. As we approached the hotel, Jim and I carefully scanned the area hoping to catch a glimpse of Maria. No luck. Where the hell was she?

At the hotel desk we asked again if she had been around but the clerk just smiled and said: "No problem, we've got plenty of *Stars and*

Stripes newspapers now," and pointed to a stack on the counter. A small, handwritten sign said "35 cents or 300p." He handed one to Jim, then turned to me.

I asked Jim if he was going to do the crossword and when he shook his head I said I'd just read his. Lord Jim cracked a (now) rare little smile and mimicking Maria, said: "You cheap sumbitch!"

The clerk had a puzzled expression on his face that grew deeper when Jim picked up another copy and handed it to me. Jim dropped two quarters into the guy's hand and said: "Keep the change." The clerk mumbled something about thirty-five cents but when Jim gave him a black look he shrugged his shoulders and turned away.

While Jim waited for his elevator I looked at both of us in a nearby mirror. "We could sure use a couple of haircuts," I said. Jim replied: "It can wait. Besides I hate going to a strange barber." I agreed. Then after a pause added: "The guy I go to at home is a really good friend of mine. We go fishing a lot. I can't wait to get home and do some of that. You gotta come out some time and go fishing with us." My mouth was running over. I think I was afraid Jim would disappear like everyone else if I let him out of my sight. When I realized what I was doing I felt a bit silly. His elevator arrived and I said I'd see him later. I went up the stairs to my room.

Once again the news room was nearly empty. As the war drew closer to Saigon I was sure anyone in the news business found an ever-increasing workload. Also, I was pretty sure Peter Collins was deeply involved with getting his in-laws to a safe haven, somewhere.

I let myself into my room and made a beeline for the bathroom. No luck! Hiram was nowhere to be seen. I wondered if he'd become a gourmet treat for a rat or had possibly taken a fatal hit from a maid's spray can or broom. I still have no idea of the normal life span a cockroach enjoys but I think Hiram really enjoyed his time as my roommate. Maybe he'd show tonight or in the morning.

I sipped warm beer and munched a cracker as I sat and gazed out the window and listened to the busy hum of foot and motor traffic. I closed my eyes and tried to imagine what it would sound like after the commies took command. A lot quieter, I was sure, and maybe an occasional angry shout would replace the occasional tickle of laughter.

Oops! I must be relaxing. I almost spilled the last of my beer when I dozed off. I drained the bottle and flopped down on the bed. Just a few minutes nap and I'll be good as new.

Bump ... bump ... bump ... hm? Damn! 10 PM and here I am fully dressed trying to wake up. Something had definitely happened to me mentally, physically, or both. I'd obviously slept for hours but I was still very tired.

I managed to make it to the bathroom sink. After rinsing my mouth and wiping my face with a cool damp cloth, I went back to the desk and opened a tin of sardines. One wasn't enough so I opened another, the last one in my little pantry. I finished that with more crackers then washed it all down with a mouthful of bourbon and a glass of water.

After sitting by the window and celebrating the onset of my last curfew in Saigon, I tired of counting artillery rounds, undressed, and crawled back into bed. I don't think even a minute had passed before I was once again sound asleep.

Good luck Hiram. It was fun.

25 March 1975 (Part 2)

South Vietnam: Panic has turned almost more deadly than the shells of NVA artillery. The airport and waterfront at Danang are paralyzed by vast numbers of terrified civilians and leaderless soldiers. Some try the road south and a lucky few are plucked from the fringe of this open-air insane asylum by helicopters. Overcrowded ships and barges, tossing in the rough water, are crushing those who try to leap aboard but fall short. Babies are thrown to anyone aboard who will catch them.

A burble of light but sharp turbulence interrupted my nap. I could see we were embedded in clouds and no doubt there was a thunderstorm or two nearby. Jim was still sleeping soundly.

I looked toward the rear and I noticed the medical attendant and our stewardess friend were having a serious conversation with the Chinese co-pilot (Blue 46). The stewardess came forward and as she passed me I could see tears brimming. She gave me a sad look and ever so slightly shook her head. She said something to the steward and using a key he let himself into the cockpit.

The young pilot followed the medical attendant aft and stood for a while looking down at his Captain, and no doubt, friend.

He turned and when he saw my concerned expression came up to where we were seated. He crouched down beside me and said: "He is dead now."

Trying to stay in control, he closed his eyes tightly but the tears came anyway. I put my hand on his shoulder and he grabbed my arm. After a few minutes, he slowly stood and returned to his seat.

I looked at Lord Jim. He was awake now and staring intently outside though there was nothing to see but clouds. Then I noticed the wet spots on the front of his shirt and a large droplet about to fall from his chin. A few passengers were staring but they weren't curious ... they knew.

The baby behind us had stopped crying.

I had planned on properly saying goodbye to our fellow airlift pilot after we landed at Kai Tak airport in Hong Kong. I hadn't planned on the usual rush of passengers getting off the airplane so they could stand on the tarmac in the heat while waiting for shuttle buses to the terminal. Everyone was packed tight in the aisle lined up for the forward exit. The rear air stair was open but an ambulance crew occupied that while removing the Blue 46 Captain's body.

I finally managed to stand in the aisle and looking aft I caught the eye of our friend as he was leaving. I waved. He raised his hand, hesitated, then stood up straight and gave me a crisp salute. I returned one of my own and he turned away. I never saw him again.

Lord Jim and I finally planted our feet on Hong Kong soil and with very mixed and strong emotions we realized we were officially out of ... "our war."

Epilogue

Lord Jim and I made our way to our respective homes and families without too much trouble. Later, when we had a chance to compare notes, we found we shared an odd reaction to our little adventure. The war zone was our real home and where we were now was a fantasy land. If there's a head doctor out there with combat experience please call me collect asap.

We also shared a feeling of utter sadness and helplessness as we monitored news of the painful and violent demise of our friends and "families."

Neak Luong was taken by the Khmer Rouge on April 1. The main KR forces immediately left for Phnom Penh to add themselves, their artillery, and ammunition to the noose around that city. A "clean-up" crew remained behind. People who heeded the call to surrender were beaten, hacked, or shot to death. Buildings were then systematically set on fire and those who escaped the flames were beaten, hacked, or shot to death.

After running over a large piece of shrapnel, one of Phnom Penh Nancy's tires exploded during takeoff at PP. This caused major damage to a wing flap assembly. Grant Swartz sent her to Hong Kong for major surgery, then like Jim and I, she returned to normal airline operations.

On April 10, President Gerald Ford presented a "State of the World" speech. He passed on the dictates of the majority in the U.S. Congress. Our Cambodian boss man finally had an answer to his question: "When are the Americans (military) going to help us?" ... Never!

The 1975 Cambodian Airlift ended. The Americans at Tailpipe Bravo wished everyone well and after an emotional round of good-byes, left for Thailand.

Phnom Penh was finally and fatally polluted by Khmer Rouge troops on April 17. Everyone, even those in hospital beds with grievous injuries and illnesses, were forced to vacate the city. Death for many was quick to follow during this strange exodus to the barren countryside. Estimates vary, but eventually, from ten million down to (but never less than) two million souls were finally freed from their hunger and pain by death.

All of our Cambodian friends at the airport were publicly beheaded in recognition of their outstanding service to their (starving) fellow countrymen.

Flying Tigers' final operation in Vietnam took place after dark on April 20 when Tiger 791 took off from Saigon's Tan Son Nhut airport. Supposedly an empty flight to Hong Kong, she instead headed for the U.S. territory of Guam to discharge her cargo of American and Vietnamese personnel (many with their families) who worked for or had been associated with American companies such as Flying Tigers, American Express, etc. This is a story in itself and is well told in a book titled *Tiger Tales* written by Tiger Captain LeVerne Moldrem.

On April 30 a semblance of peace settled over the deserted streets of Saigon. The sound of North Vietnamese tanks occasionally spiced with small-arms fire and a shout or two with a backdrop of silent smoke were the dominant features. The American embassy stood flagless, empty and silent, no longer a stage for the tear-stained and frantic helicopter evacuations of the last few days.

A loud crash signaled the breaching of the presidential palace gates by a North Vietnamese tank.

Good-bye Saigon. I'll never see you again...

Fin

Appendix I:
"Last Khmer Rouge Forces Surrender"

The Associated Press
Dec. 6, 1998

Phnom Penh, Cambodia

The last main fighting force of a steadily crumbling Khmer Rouge formally has surrendered to the government, laying down arms after three decades of civil war and a catastrophic stint in power that left nearly 2 million Cambodians dead.

But the last three top leaders at large—Ta Mok, known as "The Butcher" for his revolutionary brutality, Khieu Samphaand and Nuon Chea—did not participate in the surrender. They are targets of a possible international tribunal for crimes against humanity.

"We ask for permission from the Royal Government of Cambodia to rejoin society and the Royal Cambodian Armed Forces," Khem Nuon, chief of staff of the remaining band of radical Marxist guerrillas, said in the surrender statement yesterday.

Disarming the fighters would end more than 30 years of civil war in Cambodia that began with the Marxist guerrillas' insurgency against the government in Phnom Penh in the late 1960s.

The surrender comes less than a month after Cambodian strongman

Hun Sen and Prince Norodom Ranariddh, whom he ousted as co-prime minister in a bloody 1997 coup, struck a deal to end the country's political deadlock.

Khem Nuon claimed he was negotiating on behalf of 5,000 remaining ragtag troops and 15,000 civilians, but some observers said the numbers were inflated.

The Khmer Rouge came to power in April 1975 by overthrowing the U.S.-backed government. Under Pol Pot's leadership, they attempted to turn the country into an agrarian utopia.

The experiment was a disaster economically and in human terms. Famine soon affected many parts of the country. Those suspected of harboring opposing views, or merely of being educated, were put to death.

Nearly 2 million people died before the Khmer Rouge were ousted from power in 1979.

They have fought a guerrilla war against successive governments since.

Appendix II:
Important Aircraft
Mentioned in Text

DC-8-63 Call sign: Tiger 783 or Nancy (Phnom Penh Ph-Nancy)

Built by Douglas, this was the largest, most powerful of the popular DC-8 series. 187-feet long, maximum takeoff weight was 355,000 pounds. Maximum landing weight was 275,000 pounds that, with a safe minimum amount of fuel on board, allowed a typical load of 96,000 pounds of rice or other cargo into Phnom Penh.

Other DC-8 operators:

AI (Airlift International) . . . . Saigon
World (World Airways) . . . . Saigon
TIA (Trans International) . . . . U Tapao, Thailand

Curtiss C-46 "Blue 46"

Twin-piston engines powered this WWII vintage airplane. Max takeoff weight: 56,000 pounds. Blue 46 was totally restored, a beautiful example, and painted a glossy powder blue.

Lockheed C-130 Hercules "Bird followed by a number"

Four turbo-prop engines power this amazing work-horse. Maximum take-off weight approx. 155,000 pounds. First flown in 1954, they are still being manufactured today (1998). Several were loaned to Bird Air by the USAF solely for the Phnom Penh and Neak Luong

191

operations. They flew out of U Tapao, Thailand. We never heard them on the radio as they used a different radio frequency (UHF) to communicate with Tailpipe Charlie.

North American AT-28D

First built as a trainer, this airplane was rebuilt as a ground-attack fighter and flown by several countries including France. Same radio situation as "Bird."

Lockheed Model 10 Electra

A small twin-engine airplane very similar to the one that Amelia Earhart was flying when she disappeared. Circa 1934, this airplane was operated by two Frenchmen whom we called "Cheech & Chong" because of their appearance (long hair and very scruffy). Their lack of courtesy in traffic around the airport at Phnom Penh was amazing and a constant pain in the butt to all other pilots when in the area. I don't know their call-sign as they never used a radio.

Index

Page numbers in italics contain photograph or diagram

Index